The Mindful Attraction Plan

Your Practical Roadmap to Creating the Life, Love and Success You Want

Athol Kay

Disclaimer: This book is written in good faith as a general approach to experiencing life. It is not intended to replace the advice and instruction of your own medical, legal or any other licensed providers. You should consult with a licensed provider as is appropriate to your situation. Readers hold the author harmless for negative outcomes based on following any suggestion in this book. Every personal situation is different and the advice and strategies in this book may not be suitable for you.

For Jennifer,
who believed.

Contents

For My Fans

If you've already read *The Married Man Sex Life Primer 2011*, the MMSL blog or forum, you probably have two questions...

What Happened to the MAP?

What this book does is strip down the MMSL Primer to nothing but its power core – the Male Action Plan (MAP) – and rebuild it into the Mindful Attraction Plan (MAP).

On first glance, it may look the same, but you'll quickly discover I wrote the entire thing from scratch, eyeing simplicity and positive focus on what you need to do.

It's also for both men and women, takes a whole life approach and is vastly more user-friendly.

Is The Primer Pointless Now?

Nope.

There's only about a 20% content overlap between the *MMSL Primer* and *The Mindful Attraction Plan*. If you're struggling with your marriage or sex life, the Primer has a ton of life-changing content and you'll ultimately want both books to read.

Many Will Enter, Few Will Swim

Writers are like baby turtles. Hundreds of them hatch, but only a handful of them survive the trip from the sand dunes into the sea. I've worked hard to get this far, but I'm also keenly aware that its fans buying books and telling their friends to buy them too that keeps me in business.

Without your support, there would be no Mindful Attraction Plan. Thank you all.

Special Thanks

I would also like to extend special thanks to everyone who has been a member of the MMSL forum. Thank you for sharing your stories and your honesty. There's just no other way to have figured out some of the things in this book without watching 1750 of my "lab rats" running the MAP and reporting what was working and not working.

Most particular thanks to @Serenity who agreed to take on forum moderation tasks as well.

My First Officer

This has been a four-year process to get to this book and I've personally staked a great deal on having this all turn out great.

I now know that four years ago when all this started, I had no idea what I was doing, yet I managed to convince my wife Jennifer that I knew exactly what I was going to do. In my defense, I didn't lie to her, but I do suspect that I had expressed confidence exceeding reasonable expectations of success.

What strikes me now is that she staked a great deal on having all this turn out great too. This isn't anything I could have done without her faithful patience and constant support.

Put more honestly, she staked a great deal in me. I'm so grateful for that.

PART ONE
Fixing the Solution

Being lonely, broke, unhappy, overweight, in a bad relationship, or undersexed are all major life problems.

If you've tried endlessly to fix your major life problems, but they still aren't getting any better, that means your real problems aren't your perceived problems. Your real problem is your solution.

Let me explain...

A problem and a bad solution, will result in two problems.

A problem and simply ignoring it, remains just one problem.

A problem and a real solution, equals no problem.

Therefore, if you've tried everything you can think of and you're *still* lonely, broke, unhappy, overweight, in a bad relationship, or undersexed, *your real problem is your attempted solution.*

Before we fix your problem, we have to fix your solution.

"The greatest and most impossible problems of life are all in a certain sense insoluble. They can never be solved but only outgrown."

— Carl Jung

Introduction

How it all Started

For the last four years, I've been working on a project called "Married Man Sex Life" or MMSL for short. There's a book, a great blog and a cool online forum. The book sold so well that even as a first time writer, I managed to quit my job and write full-time. If you've ever wondered what it's like to write a book and quit your job, it's really quite lovely.

The goal of MMSL is to help men to find ways to jump start their sex lives and reclaim their marriages. The concept was rather than directly focusing on the sex as a goal, I taught them ways to be stronger and better men. Then as they became better men, their wives would find them more attractive. Once they were attractive, getting some sexy time with their wife would be so much easier. It worked really well. Many happier guys, saved marriages, intact families, affairs headed off at the pass and so on.

To my surprise, even though MMSL aimed directly at men, the fact that my advice works so well resulted in an influx of women wanting help too. Both men and women struggle with their relationships and sex lives. Over time MMSL has become increasingly co-ed and 90% of my advice works the same for women as it does for men. Become more sexually attractive and you'll get a better sexual response.

Sounds simple right? Well almost...

I've discovered two basic problems with MMSL that led to this book.

Problem #1 Structural Attraction

MMSL wasn't working for everyone. It was working amazingly well for about half of my readers, some degree of positive for the rest and a tiny handful said it made things worse.

As an example, one of the things I suggested in MMSL was the "Ten Second Kiss" move. Half the men would tell me that it worked amazingly well and their wives just melted into them, while the other half would say that it didn't work at all, or only worked one time.

After thousands of email exchanges and tracking the over 1750 forum members' experiences, I've discovered that the quality of the relationship really stems from the overall *structural attraction* between the couple. Thus, a physically fit guy with a good job trying out the Ten Second Kiss gets a great result, while an obese, unemployed guy trying the Ten Second Kiss is a little creepy.

This book is more about fixing the structural attraction issues, than fancy moves to trick her panties off. Likewise, if you really need to get your husband to the doctor, you can only trick him with a bra made of bacon once to get him there.

Problem #2 Unintentional Benefits

When I started MMSL, my sole purpose was to get married guys laid. Then the women came and they got happier marriages too. All good.

Then it started getting weird.

People would start writing to me about how much weight they had lost. This was cool, because I told everyone that hitting the gym was a good idea to become more attractive. I'd get email from people saying they lost 10 pounds, 20, 30, 40, 60, 80... then one guy wrote me and said he'd lost 120 pounds and had managed to come off his diabetes medication.

Wait. What? I didn't write a book about beating diabetes.

Along with the weight loss stories, I also started getting emails about people finally getting promotions at work, increasing sales numbers, getting a new job for more money, one guy said he tripled his annual income.

Okay, that's fabulous, but I didn't write a book about making more money.

I've also had dozens of emails about people getting on better with their same sex friends, co-workers and parents. The boss at work is suddenly a lot nicer. In addition, the kids now behave better too.

Well, I did write a little bit about parenting, but it's still better results than I honestly expected.

Want more? I know of two of my readers that went back to school and "finally got their doctorates". A fair number of people reported coming off psych meds, and nearly everyone mentions some variant on being happier, more confident and more relaxed about life.

Not for nothing, but if someone could write a book about how to get laid, lose weight, make more money, have the kids behave better and just be all around happier, well that would be an amazing book and they would probably do *very* well for themselves.

I realize that sounds rather selfish, but it's not. What I want is to be in a positive feedback loop where the more people I help, the more money I make and the more money I make, the more people I can help.

Sending positive energy out into the world and having it come back as an income source is a *side effect* and side effects are very important.

Then it hit me. The positive side effects kept happening all the time and to everyone. What I was seeing as unintentional benefits, were really the *intentional* side effects each individual person wanted. I had the answer!

Solution #1 Energy Side Effects

Getting the love, sex and happiness you want are the side effects of having high personal energy.

You cannot directly gain love, sex and happiness. In fact, the harder you work on trying to become loved, sexed and happy, the worse things tend to get. The greater your sense of need, the lower your personal energy is and the harder you push love, sex and happiness from your life.

If you look for love, you will not find it. If you seek out sex, you will not get the sex you want. If you try to be happy, happiness will elude you. The more you want to be loved, sexed and happy, the less loved, sexed and happy you are. The more you focus negative emotion and frustration at a personal problem, the harder it becomes to resolve. Your negative energy makes the situation worse.

The good news though, is there are direct ways to increase your personal energy. Once you have that in place, the side effects of love, sex and happiness start to happen. In addition, you already know what most of those things you need to do are. I'm just here to connect the dots so you see the big picture and guide you on your way.

Oh and there are no magic crystals, tin-foil hats or incantations you'll be saying. You will have to clean your room and go to the gym though. There will still be laundry that needs doing.

Solution #2 Energy Comes in Sets

If you pay close attention, you'll start noticing that many seemingly unrelated events link together in a loose set. An example of sets could be something like:

High school, living with parents, first girlfriend, crappy car, burger flipper.

College, living in a dorm, more serious girlfriend, cheap car, internship.

First real job, apartment, cohabiting, nice leased car, graduate studies.

Promotion at work, house, married, new car, completing graduate study.

In the example sets above, as soon as you get your first real job making decent money, suddenly you can afford moving into an apartment. Once you're in an apartment, that makes having someone move in with you possible. Then with shared income you can afford a better car. Then you're encouraged to keep going to school part-time. It all comes as a set.

While that passage to upward mobility is easy to understand, it's harder to see that even at a particular phase of your life, you have positive and negative energy sets at work. Example:

Dead sex life, broke, messy house, serious health issues, depression.

Poor sex life, scraping by, untidy house, minor health issues, unhappy.

Good sex life, saving some money, clean house, good health, happy.

Great sex life, excess income, house cleaners, excellent health, joyous.

Here's a time management / success set example:

No goals, lacking priorities, no work, anxiety.

Hazy goals, poor priorities, pointless work, stress.

Clear goals, set priorities, sustaining work, calm.

Motivating goals, clear priorities, meaningful work, confidence.

All it takes is one of those factors in a different energy set to come into play and it makes all the other factors in that set more likely to happen. That factor can be a positive one or a negative one too, there's nothing like a job loss (a negative factor) to create marriage stress (a second negative factor) which turns into depression (a third negative factor).

This effect explains why people reported to me that all manner of positive things happened in their lives. There was in retrospect a lot of the "Which came first, the chicken or the egg?" effect between them having lost weight, making more money, fixing some other issue and their sex life coming together. As they fixed one area of their life, other areas started clicking into place to match the more positive energy set.

11

Solution #3 Don't Force the Problem

The concepts of (1) things being resolved as a side effect and (2) energy coming in sets, leads to (3) not trying to force a solution to your primary problem. Instead, you work on raising your overall energy levels to the next set and use the assistance of the higher energy set to help solve your primary problem.

By not focusing negative energy on the primary problem, you actually experience less negative energy and start to feel a little better. If your problem was not enough sex for example, instead of stewing in a rage that sex wasn't happening, you could go work on other areas of your life. You could go to the gym and work out, fix the house, start a hobby and so on, all things that were going to raise your personal energy levels.

Then once your energy levels are higher and you're less needy about sex, very likely the sex starts to come far more easily without much additional effort.

It's the same effect with people who struggle to lose weight. Their entire life can be about trying to lose weight, what they are eating, what they are not eating, what diet plan works, what clothes fit or don't, how they feel bad about the weight and on and on endlessly.

Instead, they'd be better off mindfully seeking to improve their whole life. They could start by cleaning the house really well, making some new friends, starting a hobby, helping out in a community group, generally exercising and finding ways to save money. Then come back to the weight issue with greater positive energy.

It doesn't matter what you work on, just as long as you are doing something positive to improve your overall energy levels.

"Getting the love, sex and happiness you want are the side effects of having high personal energy."

Solution #4 Mindful Attraction

Being mindful is a way of living where you become conscious of yourself as being an active participant in your own life. There are three parts to this.

The Past: You see the past not as something that happened to you, but as something you helped create by your own actions. You see the past as something that informs you of who you are, but does not define who you are.

The Future: You see the future as something that will not simply happen to you, but as something you can influence by your own actions. That being said, you become so confident of your own ability to be attractive, that you do not set your heart on any one version of the future. Once you are more attractive, you're likely to have a better future than you can possibly plan for now.

The Present: The past is already gone and the future never really comes, the only thing you really experience is right now. Focus on what is happening right now and how you can live positively right now. Learn to gain enjoyment from being fully present and performing attraction building actions in the moment.

It's not that getting there is half the fun, it's that you never really get there anyway, so all the joy is in the journey.

"It doesn't matter what you work on, just as long as you are doing something positive to improve your life and energy levels."

13

The Mindful Attraction Plan

Tying those four solutions together is the Mindful Attraction Plan, a.k.a. "The MAP".

I'm going to teach you about working on six key areas of your life that are going to raise your energy levels and bring happiness into your life as a *side effect* of that energy. The six areas of your life are:

(1) Your physical health and fitness
(2) Your money and material possessions
(3) Your ability to attract the opposite sex
(4) Your ability to make people feel loved
(5) Your personality, fun and dreams
(6) Your experience of sexuality

The second half of the book describes a very specific set of steps to bust through intolerable blockages in your life. If you have a truly toxic partner, terrible work environment, dysfunctional parent or something of a similar level of stress, this part of the book is for you.

I want to be honest though, I'm not offering a quick fix here. Some of this stuff might take several months or even years to resolve the way you want it to, but I can promise that if you apply yourself, it will work. The bigger the hole you've dug for yourself, the longer it will take.

As thousands of my readers can attest, when they ran their MAP solely to try to improve the sex in their marriage, their entire life got better. This isn't a gimmick; this is already a proven plan of action, it just takes time.

"As you fix one area of your life, the other areas will start clicking into place more easily, to match the more positive energy set."

14

Chapter 1 – How Personal Energy Works

How Do You Feel?

As I said in the introduction, we're not going to be doing things with magic crystals and tin-foil hats. This is all going to be quite down-to-earth stuff.

Nor do you have to believe a mystical energy field surrounds us and binds the universe together. It won't hurt if you do believe that, but it's not going to be much help either.

Personal energy all comes down to *how you feel*.

If something makes you feel good, then you're gaining positive energy.

If something makes you feel bad, then you're experiencing negative energy.

Some examples...

If you walk into a beautifully decorated, spacious and clean room, you feel good about being in the room. You feel more positive. However, if you walk into a smelly, cramped, filthy room, you feel bad about being in that room. You feel more negative just by being in the room.

If you go to the gym and work out, it's tiring being there, but the more you get in shape the better you *feel*. Going to the gym will raise your energy levels. If you sit on the sofa all day eating junk food, it's fun for a while, but you'll get fatter and start to feel bad. Being a couch potato will drop your energy levels.

How you feel really matters. In every medication drug trial, a group of people get a sugar pill instead of the medication. Yet as a group, they generally report some improvement in their medical condition. They all feel better for thinking they might have gotten the test medication, so

15

they actually start to feel better in reality. The most magically effective medication in all of human history seems to be those sugar pills they give in drug tests. They help cure everything they're given for!

Feelings Are Infectious

Have you ever had the giggles? If a group of people has the giggles, they might have started laughing about something funny, but then it just spirals and the giggling doesn't stop. However if a new person joins the group, they haven't even heard the original joke, but there's so much laughter happening in the group they start laughing anyway.

Yawns are the same. One person starts yawning, and it spreads like a wave to everyone else in the room. You're probably going to yawn right now just reading about yawning. It's that infectious.

We all know a grump who could find a way to complain about winning the lottery, who sucks energy from every room they are in. Some people are the complete opposite and are just bubbly rays of sunshine and joy; when you're with them, you can't help but feel better.

Energy is Sexy

The higher your personal energy is, the more sexually attractive you are.

Think about the most attractive person you know for a minute. "Looking good" is part of what makes up being attractive, but I'm talking about the very most attractive person you know, who can just pull opposite sex attention onto them just by being in the room.

They are probably in good physical shape, dressed well, verbally engaging, fun, a little flirty, confident, smart and have a positive mood. All those things create positive energy. When you look at your sexy friend, they have a very high personal energy about them and they feel good about themselves.

You need to hear that again... *they feel good about themselves.*

Feelings are infectious, so... *you feel good about them too.*

Now think of the most horribly unattractive person you know. Someone you dread spending time with. They are probably in bad physical shape, dressed poorly, verbally annoying, turn every conversation onto their unsolvable personal problems and have shockingly bad luck. They aren't even grumpy, simply a dour vacuum, a black hole of happiness. They feel terrible.

So... *they feel terrible.*

Feelings are infectious... *you feel terribly unattracted to them.*

Your appearance is at work making other people attracted to you, but your mood and feelings are an additional layer of attraction or disinterest. The better you feel about yourself and the higher your personal energy is, the more attractive you will be to people. It's sexy!

The Stronger You Feel

The stronger your feelings are, the louder you broadcast them to the world.

Have you ever been in a restaurant when a young couple, completely besotted with each other, comes in and sits down? Their intense feelings of love start to fill the restaurant and every head eventually turns their way. If you look at them, it's hard not to feel happy for them, which makes you feel happier too.

Likewise, when someone is mildly angry, you notice it, but when someone is livid, the rage floods off them and everyone around them is acutely aware of their feelings. They don't even need to be yelling or breaking things for you to know, because you can feel the tension in the air.

The stronger you feel positively about yourself, the more you influence people to like you. It's important for people to find you attractive and likeable because that's what gets you the first date with someone special, or the promotion, or the second chance to make something right.

The concern is also that if you feel terrible about yourself, the stronger you feel that, the harder you push people away from you. It works both ways.

There's an Energy Ranking System

The higher your personal energy, the more attractive you are. The lower your personal energy, the less attractive you are. When people talk about the one to ten scale of hotness, what they are talking about is how much personal energy someone has, as much as they are talking about how their body looks.

Some people are 10s, some are 9s, some are 8s... all the way down to 1s.

In terms of romantic relationships, the 10s pair off with each other, the 9s with the 9s and the 8s find the 8s... all the way down to the 1s and the 1s.

Thus the more attractive and high-energy you are, the more attractive your romantic partner is likely to be.

The Hottest One Makes the Rules

Being completely honest here, we all have a good idea of exactly where we rate on the one to ten scale and where everyone else stands as well. If you've ever seen a relationship couple where one person is clearly hotter than the other one, you can always tell that the hot one is in charge of the relationship.

Say a woman is a clear 8 and her boyfriend is just a 7. If he doesn't do everything she says when she says it, she can always punt him from the relationship and find a man who is an 8 to replace her boyfriend. She risks no real loss by making endless demands of her boyfriend, because she can do better.

The same works when a man who is a 9 makes a date with a woman who is a 7. He controls the date and can make quite up front sexual requests of her, because unless she complies, she feels there will be no hope of a second date.

Relationships rarely last where half the couple is vastly hotter than the other is. There's always the temptation for the hotter partner to leave and be with someone more appealing. There's always the risk the insecurity of the less attractive partner can overwhelm them and they blow things up, rather than face a straight up dumping.

Being Attracted isn't a Choice

When you see an attractive member of the opposite sex, you have no rational choice over being attracted to them.

What you do with that attraction is a choice that you can make, but you have no control over desiring that other person. It's not as if men look at a wonderful display of cleavage and have a rational discussion in their heads about it. *"Oh my, those are very proportional, ample breasts, and delightfully framed by the plunging neckline on that dress. Excellent skin tone too. I believe I should make myself become aroused."*

No, they just look at nice cleavage and drool. They can force themselves not to stare into the cleavage, but they have no conscious control over wanting to stare.

The other half of that equation, though, is that if you aren't attracted to someone, you can't wish yourself to be attracted. If a wife is married to an obese, broke, lazy, smelly half-ogre, she can make herself have sex with him, but she cannot make herself *want* to have sex with him. In fact making herself have sex with him probably makes her want him even less.

This is why women with husbands they don't want to have sex with, have 101 excuses to avoid sex.

Do you really think she's that mad about the way you folded the laundry?

Do you really think the dishwasher being stacked wrong ruined her entire evening so much she had to go to bed an hour early?

Do you really think she keeps forgetting to come to bed with you because she just was all caught up with messing around on Facebook?

The neurotransmitter dopamine triggers when you look at someone of the opposite sex who is highly attractive. Dopamine is the "fun and excitement" neurotransmitter that gives you pleasure and motivates you to do something. It's a chemical signal in your brain saying, "go get with that person" and it's hard-wired into us to react as we do.

Sexual attraction for someone else isn't a choice; we all have a responsive desire. You can't feel attracted to someone unless they are attractive. You can certainly love them and be kind to them, you just can't feel attracted to an unattractive person. This is why a man tanking his career, or a woman ruining her looks, can so badly damage their primary relationship.

Unhappy Orbiters

The "hottest one makes the rules" effect is strongest in situations where the energy difference between the two people is so great, the hot one can't even imagine having sexual feelings for the less hot one. Meanwhile the less hot one feels enormous desire for the hot one. They then endlessly float around the hot one in a loose orbit, vainly hoping for the day that they finally show interest.

The hot one is always seeing someone else more attractive though. They always pretend they don't know the less hot one likes them romantically, but they always know they do. They tolerate their orbiter as a convenient backup plan should their current relationship fail.

Works on Both Men and Women

The great thing about being sexy and feeling high personal energy, is that even though it's a sexuality thing, it still works on both men and women.

Any time you see a friendship between a hot girl and her less attractive female friend, it's always the hot girl leading the friendship. If she wants to go clubbing, they go clubbing. If she wants to go to the movies, they go to the movies. If she wants to have an evening bawling her eyes out because she has no date on a Friday, her less attractive friend will be right there for her with tissues, ice cream and soothing words.

This works the same with guys. Have you ever noticed how it's always the most attractive guy on the team who becomes team captain? Same deal with the hot male and a less attractive male friendship. When they go out looking for girls, the hottest guy goes for the hottest girl. Meanwhile the less attractive guy gets to play the wingman role and chats up the hottest girl's friend.

We're all affected by how sexually attractive everyone else is. Therefore, while it may make little immediate sense, it is in fact exactly true that when you become a hotter, more energetic person, your boss at work notices it. They start liking you better and respecting you more and that's why you get the promotion over the next person as much as anything.

I mean have you ever made a purchase somewhere, for no other reason than the person serving you was incredibly sexy? You just had to spend some extra time with them and if all you had to do was pull some money out of your pocket, that was fine. Then you walk away from the store with your $97 worth of cosmetics and start formulating a plan to say it was a gift for your wife.

This is why seemingly unrelated things like going to the gym can make you a better salesperson. You look hotter, you feel better, your customer feels better about you, they feel better, then they buy something they wouldn't have bought from you before. Then your previously cranky boss starts praising you because *"you're finally putting the sales material into practice like we taught you to"*.

Energy Sets and Momentum

Remember how in the introduction I said energy comes in sets? This is really important because once you start having critical negative events like a surprise job loss, even if your whole life is going well, the concern is that other things are going to start heading in a downward direction too.

A job loss can easily turn into a few missed credit card payments, which results in a credit score drop, which a year later makes getting a mortgage much harder, which means you don't get the house unless your husband cashes out some retirement savings, which makes him mad... and so on and so on.

I realize that chain of events is a little dramatic sounding, but the concern is that when you have a personal situation heading in a downward direction, that's extremely serious even if your life is currently good. It's not where you are, it's where you're going that matters.

Likewise, all it can take is a few "lucky breaks", some extra effort and you have an extra $2000 to spend a year. When people imagine life changing amounts of money, they always imagine millions of dollars, but consider what just $2000 can do for a relationship if you're the husband.

You could pay for a gym membership, have several moderate nights out, buy a couple nice shirts and even have enough for a weekend getaway. All of which could thaw your relationship with your wife even further as you get the rest of your life back under control. Then because your wife is back into you again, when Mr. Jerk at her work makes a move on her, she tells him to get lost.

If you don't have that extra $2000 worth of positive attitude and fun together, it's far more tempting to her when Mr. Jerk makes his move.

So again, all very dramatic for effect, but it's not where you are, it's where you're going that matters. Once started the momentum or your relationships and energy will carry you in the direction you're headed.

This is why it's critical not to simply ignore something causing a downward momentum in a good relationship. It's a good relationship today, but the downward momentum means it will turn into a bad relationship in the future. It never gets better by itself, you always need to put the effort in to change direction and chart an upward momentum.

Group Energy

Something else to be aware of is that groups of people start to solidify their overall energy level. The bigger the group, the harder it is to change the energy level.

If you're just an Average Joe in a toxic workplace of a thousand employees, making it better means trying to change the energy levels of a thousand people. You're going to find it much easier to find a new job working for someone else with a good environment, than to try to change the entire company ethic where you are.

There is also the issue where like attracts like and positive people gravitate toward each other, as do negative people. A group of negative people creates a solid mass of negativity and a group of positive people likewise makes a mass of positivity. Attempts to change the energy state of the group can be meet with the active resistance of the entire group.

On the other hand, you can have a huge influence on your family. It's a smaller emotionally intense group, but you play a much larger role in it. Likewise, if you're the CEO of a company, you're going to have vastly more influence over the workplace energy level than anyone else does. It's much easier changing yourself or smaller groups of people, than trying to change larger groups or the whole world.

The next chapter talks about how to start changing your personal energy.

"Personal energy all comes down to how you feel. If something feels good, you're gaining energy, if it makes you feel bad, you're losing energy."

Chapter 2 – Three Energy States

Active Maintenance

The bad news about energy is that it always tends to ebb slowly away unless you're paying active attention to trying to maintain it. You can have a wonderful garden planted, but if you stop tending it, the weeds will start creeping in and choke out the good plants. Leave it long enough and it will turn into a tangled jungle.

It's fine to have a rest day here and there, but sitting on the couch forever just makes you slowly get fatter and lazier. Then you don't feel like doing anything and nothing is fun anymore anyway.

If you aren't actively doing anything to maintain important areas of your life – like your marriage – that area of your life slowly loses its structural integrity. Just like having a job, it doesn't matter how great you were in the beginning, start slacking off for long enough and your boss will fire you eventually.

Energy is always doing something, it never just waits for you to come back and pay attention to it.

Three Energy States

Energy comes in three basic states – Draining, Stagnant and Flowing.

Draining Energy is like a dry riverbed. Draining is very bad as something is actively siphoning energy from you and you're getting next to nothing back from the situation.

Stagnant Energy is like a dirty pond. Stagnant is not as bad as being drained, but it's not good either. Usually the situation is functional, but it's far more annoying to complete the task than it needs to be. Usually you can point to something blocking the possible positive Flow of energy and say, *"If that wasn't here, this would be so much better"*.

Flowing Energy is like a river. Flowing is the good, positive energy state. When things are Flowing, everything seems easier and more fun.

Draining Energy is like having a flat tire and having to pull over and stop in rush hour traffic.

Stagnant Energy is like being in a traffic jam because somewhere up ahead there's a stopped car.

Flowing Energy is getting past the stopped car and suddenly the road opens up before you and nothing is in your way to slow you down.

Red Means Stop

Red is the color I'm going to associate with Draining. The only thing you can do with Draining is stop the energy loss as soon as you can. The longer a Draining situation goes on, the worse it gets. It's like having the flat tire on the car, you can't just drive another 100 miles on it, you have to pull over and change the tire.

It's always easier to say, *"Stop your negative behavior"* than to stop it in reality, but it's the true solution. If you're an alcoholic and it's ruining your life, the ultimate solution is always going to revolve around stopping drinking.

The same goes for any other addiction. Whatever it is you're doing that's siphoning all your energy off for no gain, you have to find a way to stop.

You have to stop cramming glazed donuts into your mouth.

You have to stop spending three hours a day watching porn.

You have to stop spending more money than you earn.

There's no way around having to stop doing what's ruining your life and energy.

You have to stop, that's all there is to it.

I told you there were no magic crystals or tin-foil hats involved.

You know you have to stop. So stop.

Yellow Means Stop... or Push It Harder

Yellow is the color I'm associating with Stagnant Energy. As I said before, being Stagnant isn't a bad thing, but it's not a good thing either. You just need to make a decision about Stagnant Energy and either stop it, or find out what the problem really is and push through whatever is blocking you from it being positive, Flowing Energy.

It's often tempting to avoid making that sort of either/or decision about something that's Stagnant, but you're going to have to eventually. If you're not actively maintaining something, eventually it will run down into being Draining, which sucks.

The hard part about fixing Stagnant Energy is that it usually takes a big effort to change things over the short term and you only really get the benefit over the long term. It's the difference between making a twenty-minute trip to the river with buckets to get water, and spending three hours a day for a month digging a well by your house. It's a pain in the ass to do all that digging, but after that, you don't have to walk to the river anymore.

Sometimes though, the effort to get past something is just too great to be worth it. Often when your job sucks, it's not really Draining, it's just Stagnant because you do at least get a paycheck from it. Trying to fix a terrible workplace is a huge task, so you can't really decide to work on fixing all that. However, you can decide to work on yourself and push it harder to get a new qualification or a better job.

Sometimes when your primary relationship becomes Stagnant, your partner will start resisting your attempt to improve things. Just stick with it. Any time you try to make real positive changes and break free of your Energy Set, the people and things in your current Energy Set will try to drag you back to their level. Just make your changes, hold steady and often they will make changes and conform to your higher energy level.

Sometimes you just have to drop something Stagnant from your life to be able to move on. It's usually when you stop doing a bunch of things doing nothing more than maintaining a Stagnant situation and start doing a few things really well that your life starts improving.

It's not unusual to hear of people referring to their firing as *"The best thing that ever happened to me"*. Their job was likely a massive source of Stagnant Energy and the firing removed it from their life. It hurt at the time, but ultimately it forced them to find a path to something better.

Green Means Go!

Green is the color I'm going to associate with positive Flowing Energy.

When energy is Flowing, the things associated with it are actually very easy. Maintaining Flowing Energy is much easier that the effort to break out of a Stagnant situation. It's like drifting down a river in a kayak. Sure, you do some paddling, but that's mostly just to dodge some rocks occasionally. The river does the work of getting you downstream.

It only requires moderate but consistent effort to maintain Flowing Energy.

When things are flowing, that's when you feel your best. That's when you feel sexy and most attractive.

"Relationships have a momentum. You're better off being in a bad relationship going up, than a good relationship going down. It's not where you are, it's where you're going that matters."

27

You Have No Choice

Here's the kicker.

Unless you actively maintain positive energy, everything will eventually turn to crap in your life. It might slowly wind down, or it might collapse like a house of cards all at once.

Because attraction isn't controllable, even the people that really want to like you are going to start losing interest the more your energy level keeps dropping.

Unless you actively maintain your energy, actively maintain your sexiness, actively maintain your positive effort, everything in your life can fail, including your marriage.

The Energy Solution

To stop doing Draining things is hard work.

Pushing harder to punch through Stagnant Energy is hard work.

Being in Flow and maintaining it, is easy in comparison.

The reminder being that you focus on the solution of raising your overall energy set, rather than focusing on the one biggest problem.

Primary Relationship Energy

Your primary relationship is always going to be the single most important area of energy in your life.

There is a direct link between your sexual attractiveness, your high-energy levels and your ability to attract success into your life. All three things exist in a positive feedback loop with the other.

When two people who have a sexual relationship together, the energy exchange and influencing is massive. What you both do profoundly affects each other. When a primary relationship is Flowing, it's amazingly joyful and happy. When it's Stagnant, it's merely going through the motions. When it's Draining, a primary relationship is an endless grinding misery.

Your primary relationship is one of the hardest and easiest things to change. It's hard because your partner will always strongly influence you and can easily drag you back down, or sidetrack you from your goal. It's easy because you have so much effect on them you can pull them up to your new level and open their eyes to something new.

Your primary relationship being a sexual relationship will always be extremely sensitive to your overall energy levels. Your dress sense and those 20 extra pounds may not bother a friend or co-worker, but your primary partner might be very bothered by it. Only having $40 in your checking account may not bother your social group, but your partner is going to very anxious about it.

The flip side being your positive gains can please other people in your life, but deeply impress your primary partner. They will always have a deeper reaction to you than other people will.

Your career, social group and primary relationship have a connection together into a larger energy set. A happy, functional marriage for example is a positive factor in your career advancement and social group status. People react positively to your happy marriage.

High-energy, sexual attractiveness and attracting general success have a strong connection together. *They always form a nexus in your primary relationship.*

Red Yellow Green

As a short preview of Chapter 9, keep these things in mind as you read in the next six chapters.

You're always going to get the fastest gains from stopping any Red Draining areas of concern as fast as you can. After that, getting control of the Yellow Stagnant areas is the next thing you do. You turn on the Green Flowing areas as you can.

The second thing to consider is that the next six chapters are in a specific order of priority with the more foundational chapters coming first. You'll generally give priority to fixing the earlier chapter issues over later ones.

The Art of the Possible

Don't freak out here. The next six chapters are going to cover a huge variety of things to do and not do. It's one of those "easy to say, hard to do" lists. Don't get too much in your head about it, you have the rest of your life to figure some of this stuff out. Just get started.

If a situation took a decade to develop, it's going to take time to turn it around. There's no expectation we're all going to turn into Olympic athletes and millionaires by Tuesday. It's the collection of very minor gains that makes the real difference over time.

If you're in a critically difficult position, sometimes just that movement from *critical* to *serious* is the announcement of the turning of tide that calms everyone down. You don't have to have everything fixed by tomorrow, but you do have to start the process of fixing things today. Giving yourself and others hope is a powerful thing. People will withstand anything as long as they have hope.

It's really not about where you are today that matters, it's the direction that you're going in and your momentum that matters. You're better off being at rock bottom and heading up, than somewhere okay and heading down. Your relationships and energy have a momentum.

The next six chapters are a step-by-step simple roadmap to get positive momentum happening.

Chapter 3 – Physicality and Health

Feelings Come From Within

Your own body is the source of all your feelings, so taking care of it is essential.

It's a somewhat clinical way of looking at yourself, but all of your feelings and thoughts are a combination of neurochemicals and hormones racing around your brain and body. It's somewhat freaky to think that your feelings are physical objects inside your body, but they are.

Don't believe me?

Ever had a beer? As the alcohol hits your bloodstream and makes its way into your brain, your mood will start to change. The alcohol is a physical object and that physical object changes your feelings.

It's the same with psychotropic medications. Tiny little pills can make a wildly out of balance person feel and act normal and the wrong pills can make anyone feel and act crazy. Physical objects once again changing feelings.

Of course, the most famous ones are women with PMS symptoms. Inside their bodies, the hormones are out of whack for a few days and their mood tends to change to be more irritable.

Therefore, if you ever want to feel your best and have high-energy, you're going to need to take care of your body. The better your body is functioning, the better you're going to feel.

Body Agenda

The more physically attractive your body is, the better you are for making, raising and protecting babies and both sexes are keenly aware of that.

There's just no question that both men and women pay keen attention to the bodies of everyone around them. We all endlessly scan the environment for hot bodies and potential threats. It's important to realize that your sexy fit body is of interest to both sexes. If you're a physically fit man, women pay you positive attention, but men will also give you more respect as well. A part of our brains assumes anyone could become a physical threat, so we tend to be more polite to people that pose a greater potential threat.

If you're a man, that ability to defend yourself better is what gives you a greater sense of confidence, especially if you do martial arts. It's also the confidence that women find sexually attractive in addition to the physical appeal of a good body. It's a huge positive to be in great physical shape. That's why something as seemingly unrelated as working out and building muscle can result in improved sales numbers. You're more attractive, you get more respect and people feel more easily compelled to buy your product or service.

If you're a woman, let's be 100% honest here and agree that your looks really, really matter in terms of how you feel about yourself and where you fall in the social hierarchy of your friends and wider social group. The hottest looking girls get the best guys, so straight up looks can be the difference between being married to someone making $200,000 or $50,000 a year.

I'm not trying to be offensive here. Just in plain English, you need to maximize what you have. There's a vicious cycle where looking bad makes you feel bad, which creates a crappy life. However, you can always play it the other way and look the best you can, making you feel the best you can, which gets you the best life you can have.

You have to work out and get in good shape. There's no way around that.

"Your own body is the source of all your feelings, so taking care of it is essential."

32

Your Partner's Health Matters

Your partner's feelings for you come from within their body, so if they are in bad shape or ill health, they can't feel as positive about you as you'd like them to.

If your partner has an addiction, all of their feelings are going to focus on the addiction and you'll just get the leftovers of their time and energy.

If your partner has their hormones all out of whack from illness, birth control pills, menopause and so on, that hormonal imbalance is going to affect how they feel about you.

If you're a wife married to a man with low testosterone, he's simply unable to feel sexually attracted to you. No hormones mean no attraction is possible. You can look amazing, dress in lingerie and slide down a pole and he won't feel attracted to you because the low testosterone means he can't be attracted to *anyone*.

Feelings are infectious. It's so easy to internalize their problems and find a way to feel bad about yourself when your partner feels bad about everything. Be mindful of their negative feelings affecting you. Sometimes the best thing you can do *for you*, is insist on your partner getting medical attention for a health matter.

Red – Stop Slacking Off On Exercise

You know there's just no way around this one, right?

Giving an exhaustive list of things to do for working out is beyond the scope of this book, but I think it's fair to say that you already know how to get started with getting yourself in shape. You're going to stop eating garbage and start getting some exercise. If you're a beginner, that's going to be just fine for the first month or so.

Find a gym and stop eating five slices of pizza for a snack. You already know that's 75% of the solution. Having said that, weight training is vital and endless cardio just doesn't have the same results as adding weight training to your exercise regime.

However, if you're in bad shape, check with your doctor first. You don't have to start off like Rocky making a comeback. Maybe walking is all you can do at first, or five minutes of an exercise DVD. Just get started; five minutes becomes ten minutes, ten becomes fifteen, fifteen becomes twenty.

I'm so serious about this. If you've done no exercise for a long time, put the book down and go for a walk.

Red – Stop Eating Grains

Human beings aren't designed to eat mass quantities of grains.

If you want to annoy a vegetarian, just feed them vegetables. Usually what they really want to eat is pasta rather than avoiding meat. The truth is that most people are addicted to grains in some form or other. Bread, pasta, rice and corn are the gateway drugs to obesity and diabetes.

There have also been studies showing that the current form of genetically altered wheat actually evokes an opiate response in people and thus really is addictive.

A single bagel isn't going to kill you, but endlessly chowing on grains will make you fat, grumpy and paradoxically hungry.

Red – Stop Drugging Yourself

The more crap you put into your body, the worse you feel over the long term.

There are plenty of substances like tobacco and illegal drugs that are unsafe in any quantity. Stopping them is a no-brainer. However, some things are fine in moderate quantities, but start stripping your energy rather quickly in higher ones.

A single cup of coffee in the morning is one thing, nine cups of coffee through the day is another.

A couple of alcoholic drinks a week is different from multiple drinks a day.

Many people get in the practice of lots of coffee in the morning to switch themselves "on" and alcohol at night to switch themselves "off". The two drugs balance each other, but stopping both would have you feeling a whole lot better about everything in general, once the withdrawal period is past.

Have a look at the drugs you use and decide whether you'd use them if you had a high-energy life. If you wouldn't, then stop using them.

Red – Stop Eating Sugar

Sugar is fake energy.

Sugar hits your bloodstream, makes you feel great for a short burst of time, then it leaves your bloodstream and you feel crappy. Stop eating it.

The truth is most people who think they are addicted to coffee are really addicted to the sugar they put in their coffee.

Do you really know how much sugar is in your extra fancy latte? Try going without it, chugging your coffee as usual and seeing how you feel once you're missing the sugar.

Soda is liquid Satan, but then you knew that already.

"If you do NOTHING else, get in shape."

Red – Stop Eating Processed Food

The less you can recognize the ingredients on the box as being food, the worse it is for you.

In all seriousness, you're probably better off just eating potato chips where the ingredients are "Potatoes, salt, vegetable oil" vs. a "health food" where the ingredients list requires a Ph.D. in Food Science to understand.

The more natural a food is, the better you feel after eating it. The more processed a food is, the worse you feel after eating it.

Yellow – Figure Out Your Medications

Some medications are worth it, some aren't.

All medications have a cost vs. benefit ratio to consider. Some are absolutely vital, some are simply Band-Aids over your inability to control yourself. Nevertheless, they all have some sort of cost in side effects.

If you're using a medication to cover a personal weakness you could otherwise be controlling, you've set yourself up for the double whammy of still having the lifestyle causing the problem, and the side effects of the medication to fix it. The better long-term solution is to fix the problem that is forcing you to take medication.

Put more simply, if you're taking diabetes medication when you could instead control what you eat and exercise more, maybe you can quit the medication.

My feeling is that many people take psychiatric medications to cover symptoms related to simply having a low-energy lifestyle. Depression and having low-energy is practically the same thing. If you can turn your overall life around and feel better, you're less likely to need medication to make yourself feel better.

However, you absolutely MUST have the lifestyle in place BEFORE stopping medications you need. In addition, unless you're a doctor, *you're not a doctor*. Do medication changes under medical supervision, don't just toss your pills. Live the life you need to, prove it to your doctor, and then have the meds reduced or stopped.

There are just some conditions where you need the meds and that's all there is to it. If so, take your meds. I know you don't really want to, but you really do have to.

Yellow – Manage Your Medical Care

Doctors are overwhelmed, so you need to manage your own basic care.

If you have a medical condition, you need to take the initiative and learn everything you can about your condition. The reality of the situation is your family doctor simply may not know much about your particular condition, or have the time to research everything that is innovative in treating it. You have to learn about it.

Also by definition, half of all doctors are below average. If you find yourself with a below average doctor and getting nowhere in your care, you can always shop for a better doctor.

Or put more plainly, if your Testosterone level comes back as 217 and your doctor says it's fine, but you still can't get an erection, you can always seek a second opinion.

Something else to consider is finding the underlying cause of any illnesses you have. For example, it's not a perfect solution to know you're allergic to *something* in your environment and yet take strong allergy medication to control the symptoms. For a long time I thought I was allergic to "dust or pollen or something" because my doctor rightly pointed out I wasn't getting sore throats from infection, it was more likely allergies. Therefore, we started me on allergy meds but my sore throats continued...

...turns out I'm very mildly allergic to green tea. Which I was drinking because it was *healthy*.

Yellow — Find New Places and Friends

If everyone you know is at the bar, maybe you need new friends.

Everywhere you go affects how you feel about yourself and your mood. If your social group is endlessly doing negative things, then you're also doing negative things as the price of admission. If you don't want to pay that price, don't go. Find new friends.

A positive social group that helps create a positive vibe is going to be a huge boost to your personal energy levels. Whether that's your church, a hobby group, or a bike ride with friends doesn't really matter. There are positive and negative energy groups out there. Feelings are infectious, so choose who you want to catch feelings from.

Many people find themselves badly affected by seasonal moods related to the cold and lack of sun. If you find yourself shutting down every winter and becoming a depressive ogre, maybe you should bite the bullet and move somewhere warmer and sunnier.

Once you're out of a place that's Draining your energy levels, when you look back, it can be amazing how ugly and dark they seem. Even if you thought you were enjoying them at the time, your perception may change later.

Green — Be in Great Shape

The hotter you look, the better you feel, the more energy you have.

There's just no way around this factor and it's exactly why the physical part of the book comes before the other things to do to improve your life. Everything else you do comes after this one in importance. I'm 100% serious in that if you do NOTHING else, get in shape.

You're always more attractive to the opposite sex if you're in good shape. Your own sex respects you more if you are in good shape. You feel better and more confident and that's a positive factor too.

You sleep better, you digest your food better, you smell better, you sweat better, you do everything better when you're in good shape.

Green – Eat a Balanced Natural Diet

We're designed to eat fruit, nuts, vegetables and meat, so eat those things.

Even dairy products are semi-questionable for many people. If you're of white European descent, dairy products are fine in that you likely have a genetic mutation that allows you to process lactose, but maybe not. Experiment with it and see if you feel better or worse with the dairy.

Overall though, the more natural the food you eat, the better you feel. You're better off with a normal fatty steak, a piece of fruit and some vegetables, rather than anything flagged as "fat-free" or "health food". Real health food is simply called...*food*.

Green – Feast and Famine

You're designed for periods of ample food supply and low food supply.

Your body is an amazing machine. It actually expects a variance in food supply, so giving it a variance occasionally doesn't hurt it. It's totally fine to have a huge meal once in a while and shock your body into handling it. Likewise, it's totally fine to fast from food occasionally too.

I'm not saying cycle back and forth endlessly, I'm saying a big old cheat meal once in a while is perfect. It's not a problem to eat up large at Thanksgiving, but throw in some low food days too.

Keep your body on its toes.

Green – Fresh Air and Water

Get outside and open the windows. Fresh air is always more energizing than stale recycled air.

Fresh water is better than endlessly drinking non-water beverages. You're 90% water, not 90% iced coffee. Every time you drink a non-water drink, you force your body to expend energy to handle the process of extracting water from the drink. You're forcing yourself to spend energy just to flush it down the toilet.

Green – Supplementation

Concerns about natural foods and water are important, but it is also very hard to overlook the benefits supplements can have on your exercise results.

One good protein shake can make the difference between being ready for more exercise tomorrow, and being too sore to work out again until the day after tomorrow.

As you age, the joints can creak a little, so supplementation for joint recovery can be the difference between exercising far into the future and having to quit the exercise a few months into it.

If you're missing anything from your diet, supplements can cover that. A very large number of people don't get enough vitamins and Omega-3 oils. They can make all the difference in mood and happiness.

Chapter 4 – Money and Materials

Money is Pure Energy

Money is one of the most amazing things in the universe.

Money is what allows you to go to work and do just one type of job and then get dozens of different rewards for having been to work. I know that sounds completely obvious, my point is that you take the way money works for granted.

If you got all the ingredients to make a chocolate cake, mixed them together and put them in the oven, you'd be utterly amazed if when you opened the oven there were a set of brand new sheets in there. However, we can have a job as a baker, make money and then buy some new sheets.

Working on A gets you B... or C, or D and... well anything and everything.

Money is a store of energy. It can become anything you want it to be.

Money Creates Strong Feelings

Have you ever noticed how emotional people get about money?

I bet you're feeling emotional about money just reading about people feeling emotional about money.

If you make enough money, you can have anything you want. Thinking about having lots of money evokes all your hopes, dreams and desires. Everyone imagines spending the money how they want to spend it, so everyone feels emotional about money fairly equally.

An expensive mountain bike might excite you, while a brand new fancy laptop might excite me. We both get excited about money because money can be either the mountain bike or the laptop. Money always excites people.

The lack of money creates strong negative emotion. Not having enough money means you're going to miss something you need. Missing something you want is unpleasant, but missing something you need is horrible. We feel sickening dread when the bank account is down to $75 and it's a week until payday.

Not enough money is very stressful and a horrible low-energy state. It's no wonder couples split up over money issues more than anything else.

Physical Objects Evoke Energy

Ever have a favorite chair?

Didn't you always feel more comfortable sitting in your favorite chair? More relaxed, happier and playful? Of course you did! That's because things can affect your emotional state.

Nice things make us feel better and our energy goes up.

Broken things make us feel bad and our energy goes down.

Ever tried to sit on a slightly wobbly chair for a long time? I bet it made you start to feel cranky.

The things you have around you influence your mood and well-being, so you need to choose them wisely.

"Money always evokes strong feelings."

Red – Stop Wasting Money

Most people have no idea where their money goes.

The first thing you need to do is figure out exactly where all your money is going. You probably know about the big expenses, but there are probably whole rafts of little ones you don't really notice.

Two fancy coffees a day and buying lunch and you can hit $16 a day... five days a week is $80, or $4000 a year.

Is it worth it?

$4000 could get you many different things. That's a gym membership and better looking clothes, or whatever else you know you'd really rather have. Maybe $4000 is a nice little vacation.

It's stupid stuff like late fees. Yeah I know it's only $1.25 a day to return the DVD late, but it all slowly adds up.

Start keeping some kind of tracking system to see where your money goes. If you see a leak, plug it up and stop wasting money.

Red – Debt Drains

Debt is evil.

I'm serious about saying debt is evil. Now that you know that money is energy, you have to see that having debt is having negative energy. Simply having a debt is a Draining thing because you owe the universe energy for whatever you have.

However, it gets even worse than that.

There's always interest charged on debt. So not only is debt negative energy, the negative energy tries to get bigger and more evil. Debt can slowly take over your life like an energy cancer. If you're in debt, you have to find a way out of it.

Some of you are still paying for fancy cups of coffee you had in 2005!

The best advice is to avoid getting into it in the first place. The exception to that rule is if the debt gets you an asset that will create positive energy for you. So taking a loan to buy a business that turns a profit is just fine. Taking a loan to buy a house that creates a stable family environment is just fine. Putting a $3500 TV on a credit card is more questionable though.

Stupid debt will destroy you. It's like a hole in the bottom of your life, slowly taking on water and dragging you down.

Red – Stop Buying Junk

Everything you buy that's junk is just wasted time, space and energy.

Just because something is cheap, doesn't mean it won't cost you more than the price tag. Ever buy cheap shoes and then have your feet start really hurting?

Because things affect your energy levels, buying a load of junk will drag your energy levels down.

Red – Stop Bankrupting for Status

I know it's tempting. We all love to impress our friends and look good. The truth is that if you buy something that's really out of your price reach, it's going to come around and bite you in the butt somehow.

That house that's just a little too big for your budget is going to get you screwed when the price of oil goes up, or the water heater breaks, or you need a roof replacement.

The true danger for buying "too much house" is that once you have the house, you have sunk costs into staying there and it can be impossible to extract yourself from a property you can't afford without a foreclosure.

Red — Stop Ignoring Broken Items

Broken items lower your energy.

Every time you go to use the dryer and then realize, "duh, the dryer is broken", that saps your energy. You need to fix the dryer, find someone who can fix it, or you should replace it.

Every time you walk past the broken laundry room door, you lose a little energy thinking about it in the back of your head.

When the indicator lights go out on your car, you lose some energy thinking about how dangerous it is to be driving around with broken indicator lights. Never mind the brakes being old and the tires worn away to nothing. Just knowing about it all drains your energy.

If you have to use it, you can't just toss it away, but you do have to fix it.

Yellow — Use It, Or Lose It

I'm guessing there's an area in your house so cluttered it's become completely non-functional.

If a wall of stuff blocks off a section of your garage, to the point where your two-car garage is now a one-car garage, that's a problem.

If your kitchen cabinets have 37 different cups in them, but only 8 are ever used, that's a problem.

If you have 43 shirts and only ever use 6 of them, that's a problem.

If you have 127 kitchen gadgets and only ever use the big knife, a cutting board and three of the pots, well that's a problem.

You're spending so much time getting things out of the way to get to the things you actually need, that you're wasting time and energy.

To start removing the clutter, go through just one room at a time and figure out if you use the items in there, or you should lose the items in there. If you should lose them, either toss them or put them in the garage sale pile. You'll be surprised just how much better you feel when you reclaim entire lost rooms from within your house.

Starting with the refrigerator is a great idea. Take everything out and look at the expiration dates. You'll have stuff in there that would probably send you to the hospital for a stomach pumping if you ate them. If it's gross, toss it, wipe down the fridge and put all the good food back.

How do you *feel* about your fridge now? I'm guessing you feel good. You feel more energized. You feel happier. So as dumb as it sounds, cleaning your fridge out made you feel... *sexier.*

Clutter is a physical manifestation of Stagnant Energy.

Yellow – Make More Money

Compared to stopping the Red money issues by getting control of expenses, finding ways to make more money is much harder.

You may decide to go back to school for a better degree. You might take a part-time job. You might start studying for exams for a new certification. You might push harder on a sales goal.

Whatever it is, you know it's not going to happen overnight. In fact, some things that make you more money might take years to come about.

Money is stored energy, so more money always means more energy. It's a major game changer.

Yellow – Work Smart, Not Hard

Your time, effort and money all add up to being some form of energy.

If your current job has terrible working conditions, and you move to a different company for better working conditions, that's a huge energy savings for you. Even if you're doing the same sort of job for the same money, it's still an improvement. You'll feel better.

Ask around for business and work related ideas that will save you time, effort or money. If there's a better way to do things and you can switch over, that's a long-term structural energy savings. The way the internet changes everything is a key factor in all kinds of businesses needing to change their way of doing things. You have to look online for any kind of new solution or platform that will improve your way of doing things, both as a business and as a family.

For example...

I'm an author, but I can't stock my own books and sell them without losing money on every transaction compared to having Amazon.com handle all the retailing of my books. I actually make more money per sale just sitting at home and collecting a check than I would running around taking orders and standing in line at the post office every day.

It's a strange but awesome new world we live in. The smarter you work, the easier your work becomes.

Yellow – Get Control of Your Time

Time is money and control of your time is critical.

Time is a non-renewable resource, but you can maximize the use of your time in two key ways. The first is to cut out ways you are wasting your time through pointless activity. TV watching and surfing the Internet for example can be nothing more than an endless loss of your time for no discernible payoff.

The second way you can maximize your time is by spending money to get other people to do tasks for you. This requires you to have a reasonably high income and/or hourly rate, but it is worth looking at.

For example if your hourly rate is $40 and it costs $20 an hour to have your lawn mowed or a cleaning service, it may well be more efficient to simply have someone else come in and mow the lawn and clean the house, while you work an extra couple of hours generating income.

If nothing else, actively tracking your time, and ensuring you're performing income-generating activity is one of the easiest and most effective ways of working on this area of your life.

Green — Functional, Beautiful Things

High quality items give you positive energy.

Clutter and broken items Stagnate and Drain your energy because they make doing what you want to do harder. Functional, beautiful items give you energy because they make it easier to do what you want to do. Using them helps you Flow.

Some examples of functional, beautiful things...

A great kitchen knife makes everything you do in the kitchen easier, faster and better.

I asked for an amazing toaster one year for my birthday, because I like toast and the cheap one we had kept popping the toast up semi-randomly and I hated it. So now I have this nice toaster and every time I toast something, *I feel good*.

This Christmas instead of getting our teen daughters a bunch of new clothes, toys and snack items that they would have likely not paid much attention to, we got them just one main gift each. They both got brand new, moderately priced laptops. They use them every single day. They play with them and write school assignments on them. There's no fighting anymore for the old and dying computer and they don't bug me for my computer either.

So fewer but better targeted presents for Christmas meant more happiness, energy and reduced interpersonal conflict. *We all feel good.* That's money well spent.

Green – Have Emergency Money

Simply knowing that you have the money for emergencies will create a sense of abundance and happiness. It's subtle, but it will make you feel good.

Try to have a month or two of income available as easily accessible savings. If you can simply write a check for a suddenly dead fridge for example, it's vastly less stressful than wondering where the money will come from as you start tossing food out.

Figure out an amount of money that would work and make that your new mental minimum balance in your checking account. If it's $2000 or $5000 or whatever you choose, that's the lowest you let your account get down to unless it's a genuine emergency.

Another option is creating a secondary account for nothing but emergency money. Our minds are a little silly though, you're likely to feel better looking at an account balance of $2134, rather than $134, even if there's a barely used account with $2000 stashed in it. You just see the big number and feel good.

"Clutter is a physical manifestation of Stagnant Energy."

Green – Work a Positive Job

The money aspect of any employment is important, but the value of the work you're doing is an energy factor too. Anything that is making the world a better place, is more energizing than working for a company that is doing something questionable as an income source.

It's going to be more energizing working for a landscaper and building something nice in people's yards, than working as a telemarketer for what you're starting to feel is a scam.

Look to work for ethical people. Look for a meaningful, positive and productive job. Sometimes taking less money, but a better working environment, is worth the exchange.

Green – Give From Strength

When you give, you're expressing feelings of wealth and that's a highly positive emotional state.

There's an often-repeated idea that you measure giving not by the size of the giving, but how much you have left. This is dead wrong. Giving is best from a position of strength, where you give an appropriate amount and you feel completely positive about the gift given. If you give too much, you can cripple your ability to provide for yourself, which is terrible. You shouldn't cannibalize your entire energy system for a one-off moment of giving.

When you give from a position of strength, it's an enjoyable expression of having positive energy. Appropriate, targeted gifts can do wonders for people and organizations and generate a lot of positive energy and outcomes.

Even then, try to give gifts that aren't consumables and that will go on and create more wealth and energy into the future. It's the difference between giving someone a fish or a fishing rod.

Green — Invest in Your Marriage

In pure dollars and cents, sometimes the biggest cost savings can be spending money on your relationship. Finding time and money for vacations together can reconnect you and play a role in keeping you together over the long run. Dinners out together and fun experiences are part of what maintains a sense of fun and pleasure in each other's company.

Divorce is *expensive*. No matter how you slice it up, it's the same total income between the two of you and more expenses to cover. Unless someone has magical lawyers and a mean streak, no one divorces at a profit.

Summary

Money and material items are huge sources of positive and negative energy. You have to pay careful attention to them. Most wealthy people don't have one huge winning moment where they make all their money. Wealth accumulates by saving money here and there, and finding ways to make a little more money here and there. They pay attention to the details.

Your stuff can make you feel better, or feel worse. Good stuff is better than bad stuff or too much stuff.

"Money is one of the most amazing things in the universe. It's a store of energy and can become anything you want it to be."

Chapter 5 – Displaying High Value

Male Status and Survival

Men displaying high social status and resources engage the interest of the opposite sex.

The higher up the social ladder a man is, the more attractive women find him. A female teacher is typically going to be more attracted to the school principal, than to the school janitor. A female retail manager is going to be more attracted to her regional director, than to one of her retail clerks. This is exactly why women falling in love with their bosses are a cliché, because it's an obvious effect at work.

The purpose of having high social status is to gain greater control of resources. The school principal is more interesting to women, not just because of the social class, but because he makes more money than the janitor does.

I'm not saying all women are gold-diggers here either, but the simple realities of life dictate that women are at least copper or silver-diggers. Everyone needs to pay the bills and occasionally be able to afford some nice things as well. It's just reality.

If you're a man, keeping a keen eye on your career and social status is a key factor in attracting women. If you're a man, having women interested in you feels great and is a major source of personal energy.

Female Reproductive Wealth

Women displaying high fertility and availability engage the interest of the opposite sex.

The more capable a woman is in displaying fertility, the more attractive men find her. Anything that looks like a positive baby-making factor increases her attractiveness. Height and weight proportional women are more attractive because they have better birth outcomes. Younger women are more attractive because they are more fertile and have better pregnancy outcomes. Beautiful women have proportional, symmetrical features and are more attractive because they are displaying better genetics.

It's easy to portray men as being superficial in desiring outwardly attractive women and bypassing "inner beauty". The reality is that men are exceptionally on point in feeling strong attraction to the best reproductive options around them. A man feeling attraction to a beautiful woman is in fact the complete opposite of superficial, it's the most important thing in the world to your body to want to pass on your genes.

Modern women also often mistakenly believe that having a high-powered career, makes them more attractive to men. Having a great career is of value to her own support and goals, but ultimately a man is going to feel strongest attraction because of her reproductive wealth. So as unfair as it sounds, a good dress and lipstick are going to get you more dates than having a law degree will.

If you are a woman, your appearance is a key factor in how attracted men are to you and that is a major source of energy. There's a positive feedback loop where your positive appearance boosts your energy, which increases your attractiveness even more. Then you feel better about you, making other people feel better about you and your energy rises even further.

High Value Interests Everyone

The more attractively you present yourself, the more attractive you are to everyone.

Everyone is aware of how attractive everyone else is. Both men and women know exactly how good the reproductive values and social statuses are of everyone in the room. You're just not meant to blurt it out in public.

If you're a man, displaying high value to women also positively influences your interactions with other men. If you're the big shot in the room, all the other men will respond well to you. If you're on the low end of the totem pole and someone needs to give up their seat, it's you.

If you're a woman, having a display of high value to men also positively influences your interactions with other women. The hottest girl gets to be Homecoming Queen because she's the most popular, but she's the most popular because she's hot.

High Value Creates Social Dominance

The higher the value you display, the more dominant you become in your social group. Dominance might sound like a cruel term, but the reality is every interaction we have has elements of dominance and submission to it.

On a bus, the bus driver is dominant and the passengers are submissive.

In a classroom, the teacher is dominant and the students are submissive.

The person who steps out of the way and lets the other person go ahead is submitting.

If you're a lower value member of the group, you can change your place in the pecking order by increasing your value and becoming more dominant. The greater your displays of value, the more easily you become dominant and people let you get what you want.

"The more attractively you present yourself, the more attractive you are to both men and women."

Red – Stop Displaying Low Value

Displays of low value reduce your energy.

Every time you say you're bad at something, give a terrible performance, or slink around other people like the dog that peed on the carpet, you're giving off a low-energy vibration. It reduces your attractiveness.

Sometimes a woman can be interested in a man, but when he finally goes to make the move to engage her, his delivery is so unconfident and weak that she loses interest in him just as fast as he talks to her. His weakness kills her attraction.

Sometimes a man can be interested in a woman, but then when complimented she unleashes such a barrage of negative talk about her appearance, that he rapidly loses interest in her. The man thought she was physically attractive, that's why he complimented her. His intent was to make her feel better and get positive energy back as a result. Instead, the compliment results in a negative energy discharge, so she is pushing him away.

Stop whining.

Stop nagging.

Stop complaining.

Stop crying about your owie.

Stop blaming everyone else for your situation. It kills your attractiveness almost instantly.

Red – Stop Emotional Tunnel Vision

Believing someone is the only person for you creates a greater sense of need in you, which is unattractive.

If you make another person, employer or social group your only imagined possible source of what they can give you, you're dependent on them for what you need. This hands them a great deal of your personal power and creates a situation ripe for them to take advantage of you.

If you make them your priority, but they only make you their option, they have complete control in the relationship.

The truth is most things and people are *fungible*. For instance, if you want an apple and you pick a bad apple, you just throw it away and get a new apple. You don't get upset about the old apple being bad, because you have a new apple and all you wanted was an apple. All apples are replaceable by other apples. Apples are fungible.

If a morning radio host quits her job, the next day the radio station isn't going to broadcast three hours of total silence. No, they are going to quickly find a replacement and the next morning isn't going to be very different. Morning radio hosts are fungible. People are fungible.

People we are in relationships with are certainly people we care about and want to love. However, when push comes to shove, if you picked a bad apple, you can always dump it and find a new apple. It's terribly Draining telling yourself endlessly that you're enjoying a bad apple. You saying they are the best apple you can ever be with, doesn't mean they are the best apple for you.

The second half of the book is about trying to get a bad apple to become a good apple, but for now start to remember there are always other apples out there.

Red – Stop Orbiting Hotter People

If the person you want is way hotter than you are, you waste your time waiting for them to want you back.

It's often the case that you can see a nice guy endlessly circling a hot girl, waiting for it to finally be his turn to date her, except his turn never comes. He's always "just a friend". Maybe he's even a good friend, but he'll never be someone she sees as dating material. So all the time he spends circling her, being her friend, supporting her when other guys dump her... *is wasted time.*

If the chances of you getting into the inner circle of a group is impossible, all the time you spend trying to break in is wasted.

You are always better off charting your own course and developing yourself further into being a more attractive person. Thus, instead of orbiting a girl, a guy is better off ignoring her and spending more time in the gym and self-improving. Maybe in a year or so she'll suddenly start viewing him differently. Maybe he'll have better apples to choose from than her.

A similar thing happens with women trying to impress the super-hunk guy they can never really get. One night isn't a relationship.

Yellow – Start Passing Fitness Tests

Everyone tests you to figure out your value.

In almost all interactions, other people accept our social status or role at face value. When we get on a bus, we just assume that the bus driver is the bus driver because of their uniform, or hat or most obviously, because they are sitting in the driver's seat. We don't ask to see their license, or inquire as to where they went to take bus-driving classes. Our assessment of whether a bus driver is in fact a bus driver, takes about a tenth of a second.

However, in longer-term relationships, there is an ongoing assessment of our social value and periodically one party tests the other to see whether they really are sufficiently dominant to justify their social rank. We call this Fitness Testing.

Most Fitness Tests boil down to two things, (1) an unreasonable request and/or (2) an unreasonable tone.

57

For example...

Someone asks you to complete tasks related to their work assignment that aren't part of your job description. That's an unreasonable request, and if you comply with it, you're displaying you have a lower social value than they do.

Out shopping, your wife asks you to hold her bag while she tries on clothes, but does so by simply holding out her bag in your direction without looking at you, and then verbally snaps *"What's wrong with you, hold my bag!"* if you hesitate to take it. The actual request to hold her bag isn't unreasonable, but her attitude clearly indicates she assumes you have a lower social value. If you take the bag, you're displaying low value.

The way you pass Fitness Tests is to refuse to comply with unreasonable requests, and by making as little fuss about doing so as possible. *"No thank you, that's your job."* Faced with an unreasonable tone, you refuse to comply until they state the request more pleasantly.

Every time you pass a Fitness Test, they will usually be mad at you for refusing them, but because you have displayed higher value – i.e. a higher energy vibration – ultimately they start to feel more positively about you. Then because you've established a higher social value than they have, they become the one in the wrong and quite often, they will apologize to you for their behavior.

It does take some time to figure out what are tests and what aren't, but it is a very important skill to learn. Both men and women will test you.

Yellow – Maintain Your Own Frame

Often your basic weakness with people stems from an internal lack of confidence.

If you don't know who you are and what you want from life, other people will easily influence you to do what they want. There's a very slippery slope from being easy-going, to others taking you for granted as a follower.

Be clear who you are. Decide what you stand for and stand up for it. If you truly dislike something and don't want to go along with it, don't go along with it.

Yellow – Learn to Parent

Kids are fabulous at testing boundaries. They are like the raptors in Jurassic Park, systematically testing the fences looking for weakness.

Kids, especially small children, are endlessly rolling Fitness Tests. They are still learning all the social boundaries, so they must endlessly test everything to discover where the boundaries are.

Thus, every kid tries to make a scene in public at least once.

Every kid steals from the cookie jar at least once.

Every kid churns up some nonsense to delay bedtime or nap time at least once.

They just want to see what you'll do when your social value relative to theirs is tested. Will you fold up like a chump in the grocery store and give them candy? Will you beg them to behave? When they spread mess all over the house, do you clean it up?

If you do, you're displaying low value and encouraging them to take further control of the relationship.

"Men displaying high social status and resources are attractive to women. Women displaying high fertility and availability are attractive to men."

Yellow — Teach "No X Until Y"

The biggest tool with children is being firm with the policy that there is no X until Y.

There is no ice cream until you clean up the mess.

There is no trip to the beach until you do your chores.

There is no allowance until your bedroom is clean.

In short, there is the demand for good behavior before you give a reward for it.

Now, think about your dealings with adults.

How often have you given someone something they wanted from you, and never got the thing you wanted from them? How often have you given adults the X they wanted, and you never got the Y?

Every time you give the X before the Y, you're displaying lower value. Every time you act like a sucker, you're reducing your energy and attractiveness to them.

Green — Dress Well

The way you look tells people how to treat you.

The better you dress the higher value you express and the more people will like you.

The better you dress, the better you feel about yourself and the more people will like you.

The better you dress, the more that people like you, the more other people will like you too.

The better you dress, the more people will like you and the more you will like you.

Dress well. Feel better. You don't have to wait until you're in perfect physical condition either.

I'm not saying spend a thousand dollars you can't afford on a new wardrobe. Just ditch the ugly shirts and worn jeans and put some effort into your appearance.

Green – Be Cool

99% of having high value is being cool.

Being cool is all about being able to demand respect for yourself and get it, while still respecting others.

Just because someone follows you doesn't make them a loser, unless you're a loser.

So be cool.

Green – Be Playfully Dominant

Playful dominance is high-energy and highly attractive.

There is never a way to remove the interplay of dominance and submission from social interaction. If the most dominant person is you, it's enjoyable to everyone that you're providing positive and playful attention to those submissive to you.

Being funny, lightly teasing, flirting, smiling, laughing, these are all things that will greatly engage the attention of the opposite sex. It frames you as a fun and most importantly a *safe* person to allow being in a dominant position over them.

Being aggressive, angry, brooding or bullying when you lead a social group does have an appeal of sorts to the opposite sex. You are displaying high value in that you can get away with such behavior. However, aggression reduces most people's desire to get involved with you much further and evokes a fear reaction if they are isolated with you.

Green — Lead Somewhere

If you're in the dominant social position, take the group somewhere.

Most men don't realize their romantic partners frame usually them as the natural leader of the relationship. Then when he doesn't create some sort of forward momentum, "let's go here, let's do this", she starts to get annoyed with him and eventually take over the leading of the relationship, which deep down she doesn't want to do.

This is what women mean by the whole, *"I want a strong man"* line. All she wants is for the man to be able to provide some kind of reasonable direction and forward momentum without turning into a frightened little boy when she disagrees with him.

It's a very natural thing for wives to Fitness Test husbands (Yellow), to see whether he's going to qualify himself as fit to lead (Green), or going to be her orbiter doing everything she wants (Red). It's vitally important to master this if you are a man. Just bear in mind there are no shortcuts to being the high quality man that can lead a woman without her wanting to test him.

Green — Follow Somewhere

If you're not in the dominant social position and the social leader isn't being offensive or stupid, roll with what they want.

We don't all get to be in charge and someone always ends up being the leader. Rarely believe those people who say they have a 50/50 relationship, because it's usually just a policy stated for public relations.

With wives in particular you can tell it's all nonsense because when they say *"50/50 relationship"*, they jerk on the invisible leash and the husband quickly agrees the relationship is 50/50 like he's reading from a script in a hostage situation.

Most relationship fights are about nothing more than who gets to be in charge of the relationship. She wants to go to France, so you want to go to Italy. He wants the bathroom painted blue, so you want it painted green. You fight about these things just to create a pattern where you're in charge of the relationship for the really important decisions... like how many kids you have, or whether his mother moves in.

France or Italy, does it really matter? You're having a nice vacation.

Green or blue, does it really matter? You're getting a freshly painted bathroom.

Most times a leader isn't choosing between a good and a bad decision, but two good ones. So if it's a good one, just relax and enjoy it.

If it's a genuinely bad decision, then make yourself heard. If they ignore you and it all blows up, you want them to hear the *"I told you so"*, inside their own head without you having to open your mouth.

It's not always going to be you leading the way, but if the way they lead you is fine, then roll with it.

Green — Figure Out Who Is In Charge

Conscious leadership aligns the energy in the relationship.

If most fights in a relationship are about simply trying to battle for dominance over each other, that's a very large amount of wasted energy. Figuring out who is in charge creates a net energy savings and a relationship dynamic often experienced as an *erotic charge*. This explains the Fifty Shades of Grey phenomenon.

In most heterosexual couples, the man will tend to be the natural leader and the woman the follower, though there are plenty of couples where the opposite is clearly true. Also some couples split leadership over different aspects of living, i.e. I'm in charge of this, and you're in charge of that. Though if you cast your mind back, usually the true leader of the relationship approved the split leadership model, so when push comes to shove, they will usually take charge in a crisis.

Incidentally, this is something that gay and lesbian couples typically do better than heterosexual couples. In a gay couple, not only do they know exactly who is leading the relationship, *everyone else knows who is leading the relationship too.*

Even in same sex friendships, usually one friend is the leader and the other the follower. So, while there are some clear gender influences at work here, it's not a commandment to have a male led relationship.

If you're the leader and you don't have to fight your partner to stay being the leader, it also frees up so much more time and energy to listen actively to your partner. The true leader being free to listen to their partner without feeling defensive, further reduces miscommunication and fighting.

It does take a solid sense of responsibility in the leader and a meaningful degree of trust by the follower to make this work. If there is conscious agreement though, the payoffs in the relationship are excellent.

Green – Masculine and Feminine

Another source of sexual attractiveness is emphasizing your gender.

The more opposite you are to the opposite sex, the more attractive you become to them. Gender stereotypes exist for a reason and if you can play into them a little, there are some payoffs in opposite sex interest.

For men, doing more stereotypical male things like building muscle, facial hair, combat sports, cars and all-purpose rough and tumble boost women's sexual interest in men.

For women, more stereotypical female things like makeup, long hair, dresses, fashion, jewelry and all-purpose nurturing behavior, boosts men's sexual interest in women.

I'm not saying turn yourself into a GI Joe or Barbie doll. I'm simply pointing out that playing into that a little goes further than you might think.

Chapter 6 – Relationship Comfort

Wanting Love From Attractive People

Everyone wants to receive love from high-energy, attractive people displaying high value.

This is a very important point and the reason why this chapter follows the last one. If you're acting like a low value, low-energy, unattractive orbiter around a highly attractive person, you can provide them with all kinds of personal service and comfort, but they won't find you attractive because of it. They will instead see you as displaying low value and will find you even less attractive than before.

They will certainly enjoy all the positive energy and support you're funneling to them, but they won't send any of that energy back in your direction. It's as if you're acting like a reverse energy vampire by Draining yourself to give to them. This is the classic "nice guy or girl" trap.

On the other hand, if you're already a highly attractive person, they will long for your positive support and attention. You expressing interest in them becomes exciting and they become highly responsive to you. If you text them, they text you right back because they've been waiting for your text.

Seek to create a high-energy, attractive vibe about yourself, before attempting to provide the benefits of a relationship to someone else.

Touch is Love

Physical touch is the greatest tool for expressing love and trust.

Simply touching another person affectionately creates a greater mutual affection and interest in each other. Skin to skin contact evokes an oxytocin reaction and oxytocin is the love-trust-pair bonding related hormone. We like people we touch and people we touch like us back.

Though again, in terms of opposite sex interest, people only like touch from people they already find attractive. If they find you unattractive, they actively seek to avoid your touch. The exact word to cover the emotion they feel is "creepy".

Babies have an exceptional attunement to touch, and most people have a large desire to hold and play with babies. Untouched babies experience the world as a sad, bleak place and ultimately can suffer poor growth or even die from a lack of feeling loved.

At its heart, touch is an expression of positive feelings from one person to another and experienced as very energizing for both people.

Many Men Feel Unloved

Men are touched and receive expressions of love far less than women do.

Many men have their romantic partners as the only avenue of receiving love and touch. A good deal of men's sexual interest in women is a cover story for seeking touch. Men who have poor sex lives are typically struggling with a gaping chasm of loneliness as much as sexual frustration.

Most women badly underestimate the power of even casual touch on a man. Playful little slaps on the forearm during conversation are electric in intensity to many men without an affectionate primary partner.

Many Women Feel Anxious

Women want their relationship and home to feel safe and comfortable, or they worry greatly.

Women have an innate drive to create a "nest" for actual or potential babies. The bigger and better the nest is, the more they tend to like it, but if the safety of the "nest" faces threats, they also become very anxious. Once they are anxious, they typically start living in an endless, flight / fight / fright state, which is emotionally and physically exhausting. Not being able to pay the mortgage is nightmarish for women.

It's not just the physical house that's of issue, but the sense of safety and support the man can bring to the relationship. Men acting in ways that are directly protective and supportive of the women and children in their house, go a long way to making women feel relaxed and loved. Men acting in ways that aren't protective and supportive, make women feel ignored and unwanted.

There doesn't have to be a conscious desire for children in the immediate or even imagined future, because her desire for safety and comfort is always unconsciously at work.

Red – Stop Demanding Pampering

Demanding to be pampered makes you a ball of negative energy everyone else starts to hate.

You should have reasonable expectations of mutual support from others, but when you take over a living arrangement, crown yourself king or queen and demand everyone else focus a one-way direction of energy to you, you're creating a toxic environment.

It is unreasonable to demand constant attention and service at the expense of everyone around you. Don't confuse them complying with you, as them enjoying having to do what you say. Often it causes them to feel very negatively about you, and that negativity spills over to you experiencing negative feelings too. Then when you're unhappy, you demand greater service and obedience to try to make yourself feel better, but that just makes the other people in your house feel even greater negative feelings about you.

The old joke that, *"If momma's not happy, nobody's happy,"* simply means momma is an emotional terrorist, cycling negativity back and forth between her and everyone else in the house.

Red – Stop Being Lazy

It takes more energy to be lazy than it takes to be active.

Having to work around unwashed dishes piled in the sink requires more energy than washing the dishes does.

Not getting around to putting up curtains, costs more energy in lost heat and heating bills than putting the curtains up does.

Not shopping proactively for sales and using coupons costs more energy in lost money than smart shopping does.

You know exactly what you need to do around the house, you just have to go do it. Being lazy around the house creates the perception of not caring about the relationship.

Red – Stop Fighting Dirty

Routine yelling, pushing, emotional blackmail, shaming etc. are all highly negative ways of expressing energy.

It's impossible to create a positive environment by using negative emotions and tactics. The method of communication used ends the possibility of getting what you really want.

If you become a ball of negative emotional energy, everyone around you can feel that, and because feelings are infectious, they feel more negative too. If the people around you are complying with your demands out of fear or shame, it can stop the worst of their negative behavior temporarily, but it cannot begin to build a positive environment.

Faced with situations you want to change, staying calm and creating reasonably consistent consequences by your actions are the way to go. Having a screaming fit about a teenager failing to complete a chore is one thing, calmly declining to drive them to the mall until the chore is completed is another.

69

It's beyond the scope of this book to fix, but physical violence is utterly toxic. Violent people in primary relationships don't stop hitting until an outside force intervenes. If that's your issue, you will need outside assistance to get it stopped. Start making calls.

Red — Stop Ignoring People

The silent treatment, taking someone for granted, or simply being willfully ignorant of someone, creates negative feelings in others.

If you're in a relationship with someone and you ignore their genuine needs, eventually their energy well starts to run dry and they become increasingly unhappy. Once that happens, you are forcing them into a double bind where they either have to tolerate being miserable, or start seeking to get their needs met from someone else. Neither outcome is in your best interest.

The trap with ignoring people is that you likely aren't even aware that you are ignoring someone, because when you're ignoring someone, they aren't even on your radar to think about. Very often, the other person is giving you distress signals, but because you're ignoring them, you don't hear their complaints. The situation becomes catastrophic before the ignoring person realizes something is wrong... and then it may simply be too late to fix.

The only way to discover if your partner feels ignored, is to ask them directly.

Yellow — Apologize For Major Incidents

When one person hurts another, even accidentally, true healing doesn't start until there's an apology.

It really doesn't matter how long ago something happened to cause hurt in a relationship, the negative energy related to that incident continues into the future. One or two bad events can quietly sour a good

70

relationship on an ongoing basis. The solution is always to honestly and sincerely apologize for the mistake you made.

It's also important to ensure that your apology is utterly genuine, but also something you will not endlessly revisit. You're not going to let yourself apologize on a weekly basis for something that happened five years ago. You apologize once, put right what you can, and then it's up to your partner to accept the apology and start moving on. If you turn it into a groveling apology, it can quickly turn into a display of low value and reduce their interest in you, making them want to be in a relationship with you even less.

Owning up to critical mistakes, apologizing, putting right what you can and then moving forward, is the path to removing a slow accumulation of negative energy that will weigh your relationship down more and more.

I've seen some truly remarkable responses from people apologizing for things that happened even a decade earlier, which releases blocked energy back into the relationship.

You probably already know what you have to apologize for.

Yellow – Recognize Double Binds

When faced with having to choose between two negative options, draw attention to that and reframe your intent.

A classic double bind for men is a choice between (1) Working more hours = *"You're never home"*, and (2) Spending more time at home = *"We don't have enough money."*

Either option is potentially good, but also potentially bad as well. In terms of responding to this, you have to call attention to the double bind and ask your partner for which option they would most prefer you to choose. Then demand they not complain about the downside to choosing that option. So in the above example, you ask for clear input on whether or not they would prefer you to work more hours, or stay home.

Then if you mutually agree you're going to work more, they can't complain that you aren't home.

Also, as you start putting energy into trying to fix parts of your life with the MAP, you're going to have a period of greater chances of having double binds. As something changes from a negative state to a positive one, there are often shifts in the way that positive and negative energy is experienced. Understanding why that is, predicting it and keeping a frame that everything is moving in the right direction, handles the ups and downs in an overall upward trend.

Not recognizing a double bind being in play, means a simmering resentment can be building in both partners. He's mad that he's always working and never home. Meanwhile she's mad he's always working and never home. That anger can act as a barrier between them when he's actually at home. Simply recognizing the issue goes a long way to disarming it.

Yellow – Find Out What They Like

What makes you feel loved isn't always what makes the other person feel loved.

Often couples speak at cross-purposes with each other in expressing love for one another. If something makes you feel good, you tend to expect that to make other people feel good too, which may not be the case.

Some people like getting flowers, some personal attention time, others crave touch and so on. If you can discover how the other person really likes to experience love, it can often take less energy on your part to express love and get a more positive response. It can be a truly remarkable energy savings.

A tip off to learning what other people like to receive from you, is what they do for you to express their own affection. Most people love others the same way they want others to love them.

A comedy of errors is common in relationships where both people love each other, express it freely, but they love at cross-purposes and feel neglected by their partner. He touches her and is sad because she doesn't touch as much back. She gives him multiple little thinking-of-you gifts and is sad because he doesn't give gifts back. Yet there is real love between them.

In addition, because feelings drive energy so much, you're often better off with multiple small expressions of love, rather than one larger one. 360 ten-second hugs and kisses are more powerful than a one-hour massage.

People love to be truly known by others. When you give someone a gift they like, that you personally wouldn't like, they feel good about the gift and feel good about you for knowing who they really are.

Yellow – Discover the Covert Contracts

When you do something for someone else, with unstated expectations, it often turns into a negative experience.

If you spend a lot of time and energy helping someone, while you harbor an unstated expectation they will somehow pay you back, you've created a covert contract in your head. When you don't get your imagined payment, you feel cheated and upset and they feel unhappy that you've sprung a manipulative demand on them.

Nobody wins. It's a very passive-aggressive method of trying to get what you want.

For example...

Imagine you spend your entire Saturday helping someone repaint two rooms in their house and *then* you ask them for a date and they say no. It would be very easy to get angry that you spent all that time painting for them and then didn't get what you wanted. Meanwhile they feel like you set them up to get a date out of them. Though to be honest, they knew you liked them, but all they wanted from you was free labor.

73

Often what you're trying to do for someone else and get from them is perfectly reasonable, so the solution is to start turning your covert contracts into more openly discussed agreements. Then you can make a more conscious decision about whether or not to spend energy on their needs and they can make a conscious decision about whether or not they want to let you do so.

If you had said, *"Sure I'll help you paint, but I want dinner and a movie too."*, then everything is out in the open and you get to either, (1) enjoy your Saturday as you please, or (2) help paint and then have dinner and a movie. Either way you win.

Incidentally, that's also displaying high value in that you won't be willing to have them take advantage of you, and it frees you to pursue other options if they don't pick yours up. *"Sure I'll help you paint, but I want dinner and a movie too."* Just feels more engaging and high-energy than, *"Sure I'll help you paint."* You're much more likely to get the night out that you wanted this way.

Openly stating your needs very well might get you a no, but a clear no upfront saves you wasting your time and energy.

Yellow – Start Passing Loyalty Tests

A Fitness Test is where they test you to see if you value yourself. A Loyalty Test is where they test you to see if you value them.

If you already are displaying value higher than they are, you become the hottest one and the hottest one gets to make the rules. If you're in charge of the relationship, they can become concerned as to whether or not you're going to take advantage of them, or simply dump them.

If a Fitness Test comes at you with a dominating and demanding tone, a Loyalty Test comes as a submissive and even pleading cry for attention. You pass a Fitness Test by not letting them take advantage of you. You pass a Loyalty Test by expressing affection and commitment.

Mistaking the kind of test it is, results in doing the exact wrong thing as a response. In general if you're already displaying high value and they are seeking you out to get your extra attention and time, it's a Loyalty Test.

Loyalty Tests mean they think you don't care about them.

Green – Express Affection

Expressing affection is as good for you as it is for the other person.

Expressing feelings tends to intensify the emotion – angry people just get angrier the more they yell about something for instance. Therefore, expressing love and affection for others makes us feel more love and affection for that person. Feelings are infectious, so your increased expressions of love for them tend to result in them loving you more.

When you sit on your positive emotions about the other person, this starts acting like an energy blockage and it can take up more energy not expressing the emotions than to finally say them. Often in the very early stages of a relationship, couples tightly control expressing affection for each other. Neither wants to tip their hand and feel vulnerable to the other. When one person finally spills out their true affection, often the other person positively blurts out mutual affection too. Then the relationship moves into a new higher energy set of relating to each other.

Just remember the caveat from the prior chapter that people wish to receive love and affection from people they *already* find attractive. So ensuring you're attractive is an important part of this too.

"**Everyone wants love from high-energy attractive people.**"

75

Green – Say Thank You

Thanking people makes them feel good, and feelings are infectious, so you feel good too.

When someone does something nice for you, they are sending positive energy in your direction and that should make you feel good. When you thank them, it's like you sending that positive emotion back to them and it makes them feel good, which in turn can make you feel good.

Many people run their lives with covert contracts, providing you with some kind of service with the expectation of getting a positive response. When you don't thank them, you're breaking their covert contract expectations and they feel unhappy that you ignored them. However if you thank them, it meets the conditions of the covert contract and they are happier for it. They can have a somewhat negative framework, but you can avoid entanglement in it simply by saying thank you.

Put more simply, there's often a sense that it's polite to thank someone for doing something for you, and if you fail to be polite people get offended and that's a negative energy result.

Also, if you get the sense that the universe, or God, or whatever you believe, has provided you with something positive in your life, it's a positive experience to be thankful for what you have. It makes you feel better. Even if you believe pure random chance has resulted in you having something, try thanking "pure random chance" out loud and see how you feel.

"If momma isn't happy, means nobody's happy...
that means momma is an emotional terrorist."

Green – Have Integrity

Being who you say you are requires much less effort than keeping the lies afloat.

All the old-fashioned values of honesty, loyalty and trust, boil down to the one overall concept of having integrity. Having integrity means individual tasks may take more time to complete, rather than cutting corners, but over the long term, knowing you've been doing the right thing means you sleep easier and feel better about yourself.

There are always opportunities for short cuts and half-truths to flub your way through doing something poorly. To be honest, some people go their whole life like that and seem to get away with it, but ultimately the universe has a funny way of catching up with them.

If you keep doing the right thing, you never have to remember what you said to whom to cover the wrong thing. It's vastly less stressful over the long term.

Cheating on your partner can unleash colossal damage. Even the *question* that you *might* have cheated on your partner can do serious damage, and sometimes all you have to defend yourself with is your track record of being someone of integrity. Being a trustworthy partner lets them fully relax and share their energy with you. They are much less likely to hold back in the relationship.

Being a good person can directly benefit you.

Green – Most Important People First

If you have a primary partner, give caring for them priority over caring for others.

This may seem like obvious, but it is also remarkable how often instead of putting their partner at the top of their care list, the primary partner suffers relegation to the very bottom of the care list. It's extremely irksome to a wife to have her husband more attentive to his mother than her. Husbands often complain of wives treating them as a distant second to the children.

Your primary partner is the most significant external factor influencing your own personal energy. When you ensure they are doing well, you're tending one of your own sources of energy. Your primary relationship is a critical concern for your self-interest as much as genuine interest in your partner.

Caring for yourself should come first, because ultimately no one can do for you what you can, but after that your partner is your highest priority. You should expect the same from them too. Being in a primary partnership is an overt contract to care for one another.

Green — Assume Positive Intentions

Every relationship has bad moments, but often the bad moment was well intentioned.

When someone loves you and something bad happens, it's very easy to associate the negative emotions of the event with the person who committed it. So if you forget to pick me up at the airport, it's easy to transfer the sense of annoyance and discomfort that I've been stranded at the airport, and assign it to you not caring about me. The more likely reason you aren't picking me up on time is something like car trouble, you're stuck in traffic, misreading of flight information or basic failure to communicate, none of which automatically means you don't care about me.

There are always two sets of emotions, (1) the emotions about the actual problem, (2) the emotions related to people involved in the problem.

As hard as it sounds to do, it's typically best to simply work on fixing (1) first and then worrying about (2). Very often once (1) is fixed, (2) is far less of an issue.

If I'm stranded at the airport and angry and hurt at you, the first order of business is to figure out how to get me home and then we can figure out how we feel about each other.

While we fix the actual problem, it's helpful to assume positive intentions in the other person. We're just going to assume that the bad thing that happened wasn't part of a purposeful plan to anger us. By assuming positive intentions, you make fixing the actual problem easier as the other person doesn't dig in defensively to try to protect themselves. They can be hurt and angered by the accusation that you think they intended to create this problem for you and that's another layer of negativity.

On further investigation, you may discover genuine lack of care and concern for you, but even then, it's easier to take calm appropriate action when you have the original problem under control. If they always ignore and neglect you though, don't just spin a bunch of imaginary excuses for your partner.

Chapter 7 – Personality and Preferences

Only You Can Take Care of You

You are the only person in the world self-motivated to care for you.

Everyone else in the world is self-motivated too, so while someone may love you and want the best for you, they also do that at their whim. If you aren't taking care of you, there's going to be some gaps where you don't get what you need. The only person to blame for that will be you.

This all sounds very selfish and in a sense it is, but it's a positive version of selfishness. Self-care is where you seek to get the things that you need, greed is where you seek the things you don't need. The line might be a little fuzzy in the middle, but overall, if you don't have what you need, you're in a very low-energy state.

A car in need of gas is useless.

A crop in need of water will fail.

A person in need of resources will never be fully productive and happy.

It's *requirement* to ask for what you need. People don't tend to read your mind and just drop everything in your lap for you. Expecting them to know what you want and being upset when they don't, is you being toxic.

You Can't Change Your Personality

Your core personality is fixed.

You can absolutely, positively learn and change over your life, gaining skills and "rounding off the edges" of some of your less appealing traits, but many things about you simply won't change. If you're an introvert, you're always going to be an introvert. If you're someone who learns best by doing, you're always going to learn best by doing.

The things that you happen to like to do to recharge your batteries are always going to be the things that recharge you. The things that drain your energy aren't likely to change either.

It's up to you to become self-aware and know what works for you and what doesn't.

Red – Stop Nerfing Your Personality

Trying to be something you're not, rings false and will exhaust you.

The trite thing people say is to *"just be yourself"*, which is always confusing advice to most people. What they really mean is *"Stop nerfing your personality"*.

There are bunches of things about you that people might not like, so it's very tempting to stop doing or being those things in the hopes that people will like you more. Unfortunately when you do that, you also take away all the things that people might *like* about you, because the things people might like or dislike about you, are the same thing.

So when you nerf your personality like that, you just become boring and no one likes you much. You come across as dull and lifeless when you kill your own energy. It's unattractive.

Let's say you really like camping and hiking. If you purposely display that about yourself, when you meet someone who isn't interested in camping and hiking, they are at least going to find you to be interesting and upbeat. However, if you meet someone who is interested in camping and hiking, they'll really like you, as you'll have a lot in common and you'll have a good vibe.

The other thing that happens is that when you stop hiding your interests and quirks, you become known for them, which if nothing else flags you as a "non-boring" personality and people will start referring others to you

81

for your knowledge and skill, thus building a bigger social network for you and increasing the positive energy Flow into your life.

Red – Stop Fake Relaxation

So many leisure time activities are actually Draining rather than relaxing.

If it's an electronic anything, odds are that it's *stimulating* rather than *relaxing*.

You sitting at the beach with a laptop and a cell phone, checking your email, pinging messages back and forth and so on, is probably more stimulating than relaxing.

You grinding for 12 hours to reach the level cap on an online role-playing game... *is work.*

You turning a night out into a drinking binge and spending the next 24 hours wishing you were dead... *is exhausting.*

You turning a few friends coming over for dinner into a seven-course extravaganza where no one gets to see you because you're in the kitchen the whole time... *is overkill.*

Are you really relaxing when you say you are, or are you just tacking on one more round of busy work and spending mental energy to "relax"?

Red – Stop Doing Things You Hate

If you hate doing something, it drains huge amounts of energy from you.

Many of our daily tasks are simply maintenance chores that we have to do. You may not like brushing your teeth, but you just have to do it. However, there are often tasks we do that we particularly hate for no clear reason, and if there's a way to stop doing them, it's often a positive energy shift.

If you hate shoveling snow, one solution is paying someone else to remove the snow.

If you hate going on nature walks with your spouse, one solution is going to the beach instead.

If you hate doing your kids' chores for them, one solution is enforcing that they do their own chores.

There's often an energy cost involved in deflecting the hated task, after all, that's probably why you just kept doing it in the first place. Over the long term though, you will slowly lose energy by endlessly doing things you hate.

Red – Stop Loving Energy Vampires

Vampires don't kill you, as long as they can drink your blood a couple of times a week.

Let's be real here, shall we? Some people just suck. You know the ones, they see you coming and immediately have a tale of woe and misery that you absolutely must sit through, so that you can offer them thoughtful advice that they can ignore. Every moment with them slowly siphons your joy, happiness and up to 3% of your soul at a sitting.

Just dump them from your life.

I promise you'll feel better.

They only exist on your energy and while they suck it from you, they will never get any better in their own life. They probably have a little energy farm of drained unhappy minions you don't even know about. As soon as you cut them off, they'll make a beeline for an orbiting ex-boyfriend, a friend on Facebook, their brother or their parents.

This gets tricky when it's your own extended family being the energy vampires. Just try to cut the contact down to a manageable level and stop engaging them. Energy Vampires love engagement and to draw you into conflicts and psychodrama. Avoid.

Move to an entirely new city if you have to. You'd be surprised how much peace of mind being a plane flight away gets you.

The difficult ones are where the Energy Vampire is your primary partner. The entire second half of the book is devoted to dealing with such an issue. For now though, if the Energy Vampire is you partner, try to set a reasonable limit on excessive dumping of their day on you.

Red – Stop People Pleasing

Trying to please other people at the cost of pleasing yourself, only affects your happiness.

It's easy to catch yourself in a cycle of trying to please other people to earn their love and respect. Unfortunately, all that amounts to is a display of low value on your part. It doesn't actually earn their love and respect; it slowly earns their contempt. Meanwhile, you've been ruining your own happiness while you're trying to make them happy.

People demanding you please them are often seeking to exploit your energy at no cost to them. Thus, when you actually comply with them, they see you as a bit of a sucker.

If your motivation to please other people is strictly an internal thing, often the motivation is a negative one. Usually it's a fear of some kind, like a fear of rejection, failure or embarrassment. When you try to please people from a position of fear, it's a display of low value and slowly damages your relationships with them.

You can usually detect that your own people pleasing is happening when you are using negative self-talk, to convince yourself to do something you don't want to do. If you're deriding yourself that *"Only a terrible person wouldn't help out the bake sale", while* you spend your day baking cookies instead of going to the beach like you want to, there's people pleasing happening.

Fearing someone else's anger is also a tip off. People pleasing is often about a learned childhood response to try to keep the peace. Mom used to yell a lot and conditioned you to be a good girl and not make her mad. This is why even though you're angry about it, you skip the beach and bake cookies for the bake sale.

If you're doing something nice for someone and you're angry about it, you're probably people pleasing.

Yellow — Learn Your Personality Type

If you're a little lost as to who you are, you may as well start with personality testing and see what you discover.

One of the most popular ones is the Myers-Briggs Type Indicator. Once you start testing and talking about it, you'll probably find a good 25-30% of other people have already taken it too. It's a helpful tool to use to discover your primary skill sets and style of interaction with people.

My personal favorite is the Enneagram, which groups people into nine primary personality types. It's a little more time consuming to delve into, but the insights are greater. Of particular interest to me is that the Enneagram covers what your personality looks like when it's in a positive place, a neutral one and a negative one. There is also far more direction given for ways to apply effort toward personal growth.

Why expect others to understand you when you don't even understand yourself?

Yellow — Start Paying You First

Start finding ways to put yourself at the top of your list.

Depending on how big of a hole you're digging yourself out of, getting to put yourself at the top of the list may seem to be an impossible task. However, it's still important to start switching your energy framework from one where you don't count, to one where you do. Even if you start with the tiniest of symbolic gestures that you matter to you, it's worth doing.

Maybe all you can do is place your gym membership at the top of your monthly budget list. That way the chocolate lattes fall off the budget before the gym membership does.

Maybe all you can do is start scheduling a half an hour of time each evening for a walk, because that's what energizes you.

Maybe all you can do is set an expectation that each day you'll wear a nice shirt instead of a dirty sweatshirt, because that makes you feel better.

Not everything costs money, but everything does cost energy. Find a way to pay yourself your own energy first. It's a powerful way of sustaining yourself. If you endlessly put yourself last in line for your own positive intentions, everyone else will pick up on that too and make you last in line for their intentions.

Yellow — Decide What You Want

If you don't know what you want, no one else will tell you.

If you don't know what you want, you lack engagement with your own life energy, halting your own forward momentum. Even having a short-term goal that you ultimately discard is better than having no goal at all. When you get into action, the energy in your life stirs up and you start making progress. It's often when you try to go somewhere, the blockages on the way reroute you toward a new goal you wouldn't have otherwise thought of. The frustrations of the journey may lead you to a better outcome than you could have previously imagined.

There's usually very little wasted action over the grand scheme of things. Often what appears in the moment to have been a mistake, or "the wrong action", turns out to have been a critical learning moment toward the deeper goals of your life. In the long run, even the wrong action is typically better than no action at all.

If you don't know what you want, you will typically start falling into the stronger frame of other people who are seeking to get what they want. They are in action and thus have a higher energy than you do, so it's easy for them to sway you and catch you up into their dreams rather than your own.

If nothing else, write out a bucket list of things you want to do at some point in your life. This could be anything you like: things well beyond the power of your current life, things that would require incredible good fortune to happen. Don't worry about how you get to them, some of them may be decades away from where you are now. Just write the list.

Then start doing things on your list.

Yellow – Control the Electronic Devices

It's hard to stay focused on the important when everything seems urgent.

Every time a text, phone call, email, instant message, update, or blog comment interrupts you, your attention diverts from what you were doing. With every single interruption, it costs mental energy coping with the new stimulation and task interference. It's easily possible to spend an entire day simply trying to keep up with your electronic devices transmitting information to you and getting nothing done of any real lasting value.

Take the time to figure out a plan controlling the volume of your time spent dealing with catching up on email and so on. Also if possible, try to push the time you do all of that a little later in the day. If you wake up with only one thing to do – the important thing- it's much easier getting that one thing done before trying to deal with the information overload of 43 emails filling up your head.

Set some appropriate limits on the people who have direct and immediate access to you, who understand your time is valuable. If you're at work and twenty different people think it's okay to randomly text you, you'll never get anything done. If you're at work and your spouse texts you, then it's likely to be something that's important enough to pay attention to.

Unless you truly need immediate notification of things, turn off all the automatic notifications that you have set for Facebook updates, online comments and so on. Those things will all still be there when you log on at your designated time to manage them. Someone replying to your comment about a picture of their kid on Facebook doesn't mean you need to drop everything and attend to it right away.

Try shutting everything off for 24 hours as an experiment. If you want to chew your arm off in boredom, then that's a good sign you're just addicted to time wasting on the Internet.

Green — Do What Energizes You

Everyone is different, so do what recharges your batteries and makes you feel good.

If you need to stop doing the things you hate that drain your energy, then you need to start doing the things you love that make you feel better. If you really relax best by reading romance novels, do that. If you really relax best by going fishing, go fishing.

Have fun!

"You are the only person in the world self-motivated to care for you."

Green – Enjoy the Journey

Life is a journey, so enjoy the ride.

We have an addiction to instant results these days. A webpage taking an extra five seconds to load is genuinely annoying. Everything needs to be now, now, now.

We can have such tunnel vision frustration of what we want in the future, we miss what is happening now, now, now. This comes back to being mindful. The past is over, the future we imagine might not even happen, so be fully present now.

Now usually isn't that devoid of enjoyment if you care to look. Stop what you're doing for a moment and do some "management by walking about", just go see how everyone else is doing on their own journey. Don't do their work for them, just tune in and connect.

You only get one shot at life, so don't miss seeing it.

Green – Complete Tasks

Finishing tasks is energizing.

Until you finally complete them, incomplete tasks drain your mental energy quietly in the background. Every time you walk past the broken thing you meant to fix, or the half knitted scarf, or the room that was only partially painted, your energy drops just thinking about the task that needs to be finished.

The good news is that when you actually complete a task, you get a positive energy boost and you feel better simply for having completed whatever it was. So get started and pick something unfinished and finish it off. You'll feel better.

The caveat to that being, with very large efforts to finish a major project, there's often an energy let down right after having completed the project, or even just a few steps away from the finish. The final hundred yards of a marathon seems like an impossible extra mile. Just push through and expect the emotional dip. Once past the dip, your sense of accomplishment and pride will resurface.

Green – Pay Attention to Flow States

In a Flow State, everything seems effortless, you lose track of time and you produce your best work.

Going into a Flow State means that you're hitting the right combination of your skill level, task difficulty, enjoyment and natural talent for what you are doing. Everything suddenly clicks into place, as if you're the Michael Jordan of whatever it is you're trying to do. It's an extremely high-energy experience and feels more like merging into a greater consciousness than anything you have direct control over.

If you experience a Flow State, the odds are extremely good that you are doing exactly what you should be doing with your time, effort and energy.

However, you can't mentally just will Flow States into being. You can't decide to get into a Flow State. All you can do is get into action and sometimes they hit. The more positive energy you have in the rest of your life, the easier they seem to come. Skill at the task you're doing is important, and there are simply no shortcuts to gaining skills other than practicing using them.

If a Flow State hits, then ride it out until it's over. These are moments of maximum creativity and output.

"Finishing tasks is energizing."

Green — Quality Beats Quantity

A perfect steak once a week beats a hamburger every day.

I love the "Most Interesting Man in the World" ads.

"I don't always [experience], *but when I do, I* [high quality experience].

More often than not, the little bit of extra money for a better experience pays for itself in terms of your positive mood and energy levels. Sure, you could buy a cheeseburger every day as an eating out treat, or you could have a proper meal at a restaurant and get something great.

The quality experiences always make for better memories.

Note that I said *experiences,* as opposed to *things.*

Chapter 8 – High-Energy Sex

Good Sex is the Ultimate Side Effect

One of the key ideas in this book is that you can't directly fix your major life problem and your true solution lies in raising your overall energy levels and attractiveness. *Of all your potential major life problems, the sexual area is the one where that is most true.*

The bad news is that trying to fix a bad sex life *directly* just makes things horribly worse. The harder you work on fixing it, the worse it gets. You push on your partner for more and they hate you for it.

The good news is that trying to fix your sex life *indirectly* not only makes things better, it quite often solves itself with near zero additional effort. Your partner starts feel excitement for you again.

All energy factors into your baseline sexual energy. If you have a high-energy vibration, odds are you're currently also feeling rather sexy. Everybody else finds you sexy too, so it's very easy for your partner to want to have enthusiastic sex with you.

Just think for a moment...

If you were working out and in great shape (chapter 3), had a decent amount of cash and some nice things (chapter 4), were displaying high value and confidence (chapter 5), were a very comfortable and considerate person to be with (chapter 6) and had some cool personal interests and Zen (chapter 7)...

...how sexy would you be?

If you were that version of you, do you think your partner would be drooling at the chance to jump into bed with you? You know they would.

See how none of that is working directly on the sexual needs, though?

But... if you just open up the floodgates of complaint and whine *"You never initiate"* or *"I'm tired of you not wanting to have sex with me"* or *"Seriously, would it kill you to give me a blowjob?"* Well, you probably felt yourself recoiling just reading about that sort of complaining, let alone hearing it from someone you don't actually want to have sex with.

You can't just attack the sexual problems in a relationship head on without making it worse.

No Quick Fix

There are no shortcuts to fixing your sex life.

I'm deadly serious on this point. There really are no shortcuts. Oh, people will try and sell you magic penis pills, fancy outfits, toys, games, books, lotions, lubes, oils and poorly designed costumes, but none of them will be very effective unless you have everything else in place first.

You can *acknowledge* to your partner that the sexual area is something you're unhappy with, but the frame for that has to be that you understand you have to work on yourself. You can't pressure them to want to have sex with you, because as I said early in the book, attraction isn't a choice. They can't mentally decide that you turn them on. Either you turn them on or you don't.

Major Caveat, Fix Medical First

If your partner has a medical issue interfering with their sexual response, nothing you do to make yourself sexy will make them want to have sex with you.

Imagine you're an attractive wife and your husband is barely interested in you sexually. If the core problem is that he has low testosterone and cannot have normal sexual function, you can kill yourself in the gym, have a complete makeover, wear a tiny pink thong, slide down the new stripper pole you installed in the bedroom and he won't want to have sex with you.

There are also a world of hormonal things that can go on with women, most notably related to hormonal birth control and menopause that can play havoc with a woman's sex drive. If her hormonal levels are all over the place, you can look like a fitness model, wear suits made of $100 bills, kill a tiger with your bare hands and she still won't pull away from Facebook to go to bed with you.

If sexual desire is really just out the window for no clear reason, it's very much worth ruling out medical issues and medication effects early on in the process. The frame for that is, *"Maybe it's me, maybe it's you, maybe it's both of us. Let's both make appointments for full physicals and hormone panels. We can also start going to a gym and getting in shape. Let's figure this out."*

It's also worth mentioning that most people are highly resistant to seeking medical attention for things that require a change in their perspective of self-worth. Mentally ill people utterly resist starting psych medication, men with erectile dysfunction and low testosterone are harder to get to the doctor than getting a cat to the vet. If getting your partner to accept medical treatment is the major problem you're looking to solve, the entire second half of the book lays out a way to leverage toward that.

Red – Stop Blaming Them About Sex

It's not their fault they don't want sex with you, so stop blaming them.

99% of the time, it's either you being unattractive or them having a medical issue that is driving their sexual disinterest. You being unattractive is your fault, their having a medical issue is merely unfortunate and no one's fault. Therefore, you not getting sex isn't their fault.

It's very important to try to cut back on all the negative emotions and energy you express toward your partner when they aren't into sex with you. It just doesn't make anything better. You want your partner to feel positive and excited about sex with you, so sending them strong negative emotions is simply going to repel them further.

Take all that anger and head to the gym. Being frustrated and angry is completely normal and a sign that you aren't getting what you need from your relationship, but you have to channel that anger into a positive and productive outlet. Whether you're male or female, the gym is perfect for that. Take all that rage and lift some heavy weights. You'll feel better for doing it and you'll be doing the key thing on your list for looking and feeling more attractive.

It may be some time before the sex comes back online, but at least you'll know you're doing something perfectly targeted to fix your problem.

Red — Stop Faking Sexual Pleasure

Faking sexual enjoyment when you're unsatisfied just gets you more bad sex.

Ladies, ladies, ladies... if you squeal and squirm and roll your eyes back into your head, but it was actually terrible, he'll think he's king stud and you'll keep getting that terrible sex time after time after time.

I know you don't want to hurt his feelings, but at some point the truth has to come out and the longer you wait, the bigger the fallout will be from that. The longer you lie, the worse it is.

Bottom-line though, when you fake sexual pleasure, you're actively planning to have a bad sex life.

"The sexual area of your life is the one most sensitive to your energy levels and attractiveness."

Red – Stop Outside Sexual Sources

Having outside sexual sources steals large amounts of energy from the relationship.

The obvious one for this is having an affair. The person having an affair is very plainly diverting time, money, emotion and loyalty away from their primary relationship, and into to a third party. This is a truly epic energy theft and puts the primary relationship in a great deal of jeopardy. Your relationship with your primary partner will never balance while one or both of you are having an affair.

Most all readers will automatically agree that an affair is a very cruel thing to do to a partner, but many couples also experiment with consensual swinging, open marriages and threesomes. On the surface, this is an appealing option in that it's the sexual excitement of an affair, but done honestly and with your primary partner's approval. However, I truly advise extreme caution in trying any of this. Attraction is not a choice. Feelings are infectious, and when playing with fire long enough, burns will eventually happen.

The other outside sexual source is porn. While I'm by no means a prude, it's really starting to become clear to me that we are a long, long way from "porn" being some Playboy Magazines stolen from your brother's secret stash.

At its simplest, if you are endlessly masturbating to porn, there is no sexual energy left over for your partner. Also, at very high usage rates, it becomes harder and harder to find suitable porn to get a sexual response to. The combination of Internet addiction and porn addiction is very potent and simply just far beyond the design specs of a normal human being. When you've seen more naked women than all the Emperors of China combined, it's just not normal sexuality anymore. Increasingly I'm seeing erectile dysfunction, depression and lack of emotional connection as a side effect to heavy internet porn use.

Again, the core issue is whether sexual energy diverts away from the primary relationship. Sexuality is potent energy, so this energy loss is always going to be a critical concern. Without it functioning normally, the relationship will never be happy and stable.

Denial about the effects of sending sexual energy out of the relationship is very common. Just ask yourself, *is this making my sex life with my primary partner better or worse?*

Red — Stop Trying to Force It

If someone doesn't want sex with you, pressuring them reduces their interest further.

It's perfectly fine to ask for sex and even try to playfully instigate your way past a no. Beyond that though, when you pressure someone who doesn't want sex with you, all that happens is they throw their shields up and harden themselves against you.

When you repeatedly push sexual approaches on a disinterested partner, they can attune themselves to go into a state of pre-emptive resistance to your advances. In other words, they internalize the no on a permanent basis, so instead of only having to seek a yes, you've made everything much harder to do.

Some of this confusion may come from the way women do respond positively to strong confident approaches and physically intense sexual experiences. However, they only respond to that from men they are already attracted to. From someone they are unattracted to, it's something they very much detest.

If you're in a low attractive state, you're not going to get much sex no matter what you do, so you may as well make some relationship headway and stop making them so avoidant of you. Lighten up, stop trying to force it.

"There are no shortcuts to fixing your sex life."

Yellow — Discover the 30% That Works

Only about 30% of everything you try in bed works for any one couple.

Often a couple can have an unexciting sex life because they've never bothered to really explore different things with each other. It's easy to settle on a tiny handful of positions and sexual moves and then repeat them over and over until they are no longer fun.

In exploring things with a partner though, you're absolutely going to run into things that just fail. Your best girlfriend may swear over margaritas that something her husband does is utterly amazing, but when you try it, it's too tickly to enjoy. You might have read about a sexual position that promises fireworks, but all you experience is "Ow!"

When you experiment with each other sexually, you're going to have some awkward failures. You just have to laugh about it and try something else. If you keep trying new things, you'll start to stumble onto things that really work for the two of you and they will keep your sex life fun and exciting forever.

There's a world of blogs, books and educational material that can open your eyes to what you can do together. No one is born a fabulous lover, you do have to learn some skills.

Yellow — Work On Your Sexual Fitness

If you feel neutral about having sex on any given night, do it anyway.

This really does assume that you're not actively sick, exhausted or otherwise repulsed by your partner. If your partner has a whole lot of "Red" things to get a handle on and you really dread having sex with your partner on any given night, then don't have sex.

However...

If you simply feel sexually neutral on any given night, go ahead and have sex together. There's a kind of sexual fitness at work where the more you have sex, the more you want it and the better you get at it. Sex is like dancing. If you never get into a routine of practicing dancing together, you wouldn't expect the first time you dance together in six months to be fabulous. You'd probably expect it to look like two penguins fighting.

All I'm saying is get into some practice of sex together. The more you do it, the better it can get. By definition, half the sex you're going to have is below average sex. Don't expect some kind of crazy sizzling performance either. Sometimes you just have to work through a little below average sex to get to the good sex.

Even if you start out completely neutral, with enough foreplay they can turn you on so much, you'd quite like the experience by the end of it. If nothing else, you're getting into action and any action is better at getting the energy going again than no action.

Yellow — Take Turns

If you only focus on what you both like, you're robbing each other of fun.

Most couples have a handful of things they both like and then some things that only one of them is really into. I.e. they both like "A", he also likes "B", she also likes "C".

My strong advice is to simply get over it and not so much take one for the team, but learn to get your pleasure from their pleasure. You may have no interest in something at all, but seeing your partner positively writhing with pleasure when you do it to them really is fun. Eventually you'll start to like the activity too.

If something isn't dangerous or painful and your partner wants it, give it a shot at least once. If they really want something badly and you endlessly refuse, you have to consider that may have very negative effects on your relationship. If they can't get something they really want sexually from you, who do you expect them to get it from?

99

Also on any given night, if one partner is feeling neutral sexually, but is agreeable with having sex, don't pile on massive expectations of an all-star sexual performance. Many women decline neutral sex because they don't want to have to try to force an orgasm on a night they are too tired. One old-fashioned quickie is better than kissing goodnight and being lonely and horny. Many women simply like the closeness, skin contact and pleasing their partner, even if the sex *seems* one-sided.

As a caveat though, "neutral" sex doesn't mean lie there like a starfish, rolling your eyes and hating him with your vagina. If you feel that way, don't have sex as it just makes both of you feel bad. "Neutral" means not turned on, but not turned off, so warm up each other a little first.

Green — Committed to Your Partner

Don't let a dip turn into a disaster.

Every relationship has ups and downs, and times when it's simply hard going. There will be times when other people offer sex. It's very easy to turn down extra sex when things are going great, it's much harder when things are going poorly.

My strong suggestion is that you pass on extra sexual events. You risk so much for so little. Things have a way of coming around and blowing up, even years after the fact.

If nothing else, you'll know what you did. If that doesn't make you feel bad and throw your energy off a little, well that's concerning in and of itself isn't it?

"The more generally attractive you are, to the point of other people expressing sexual interest in you, the more interested in you your partner is. "

Green — Express Yourself

When you're having sex, freely express how good it is for you.

Sex is a very primal thing. It comes from deep within us and many of the motivations are well below the surface of our rational thought. It's easy to feel out of control, and one way of trying to maintain control is by clamping down on expressing how much you're enjoying it.

If you're in the middle of an orgasm and your face is barely cracking a smile, you're actually doing your best to stifle the orgasm and reduce your pleasure. It's almost the reverse of faking an orgasm, you're actually having an orgasm but trying to fake you're not having one.

You're not so much as going to "act" that you're having more pleasure than you are, but you're going to be more willing to relax and let loose on the experience. This can prolong and intensify your enjoyment.

In addition, your partner will enjoy your enjoyment of sex more if you are expressive. A lot of the emotional enjoyment of sex comes from watching your partner experience pleasure... did I mention feelings are infectious yet?

Your feeling good makes your partner feel good.

Green — Play All Day

If you want to be their lover, act like their lover.

If your partner were involved in an affair, there would likely be heavy use of texts and calls between themselves and their lover. Affair partners can send *thousands* of text messages a month. Why leave the door open for someone else to try to move in on your partner, when you could have that intimate and intense connection yourself?

If you spend some time during the day flirting, teasing, texting and taunting, bedtime is more of a sure thing. Sexuality doesn't suddenly come online at 11pm. Sexuality is on 24/7 and having multiple moments of sexiness during the day, without expecting instant intercourse, creates and sustains an erotic charge. That erotic charge more easily turns into a full sexual experience once bedtime rolls around.

Green — Touch the Penis

For most men, the only clearly understood signal of female interest is her touching his penis.

Most women are too subtle for most men to read correctly. A wife may be flipping her hair, laughing at the jokes, touching her exposed skin, licking her lips, cocking her head to expose her neck, saying she's a little tired and wants to go to bed early... and the husband will completely miss all the signals of her being in the mood that night.

In fact, he'll probably complain that she's never interested in sex and never initiates.

The easy solution is for her to be just slightly less lady-like, and rub his penis through his pants, or directly start stroking him if he's naked.

A wife who corners her husband during the after dinner clean up and rubs the front of his pants while saying *"Mmmm... bedtime in just four hours"* is communicating clear intent her husband can understand.

Green — Just Make a Move

The bull doesn't complain that the cows don't initiate.

In 99% of the animal kingdom, the male is the one that makes the move on the female. If you're the man in the relationship, odds are good that she's going to be looking to you to make the first move in escalating things sexually.

So yeah, it's great if she does just reach out and touch the penis, but you shouldn't rely on that. Complaining that your wife doesn't initiate sex is like her complaining that you don't initiate shoe shopping.

Just bust a move. Does it really matter who started it if she's got her legs wrapped around you?

Chapter 9 – Easy Fixes, Big Gains

The Order of Operations

It's time to start tying all of this stuff together. Catching up on the topics of the last six chapters...

1. Physicality and Health
2. Money and Material Wealth
3. Displaying High Value
4. Building Relationship Comfort
5. Personality and Preferences
6. High-Energy Sex

That order isn't accidental. *The higher up the list it is, the greater priority it is to address first.* So heading to the gym to improve your fitness is very much the most important thing you do.

Physicality and Health comes first because all your feelings and most of your energy are going to come directly from your own body. If your body is in bad shape, your overall energy and happiness will be low. Notice how everything in your life can be going great, but as soon as you get sick, your energy levels take a dive and you're miserable.

Money and Material Wealth is second, because money is stored energy and the material items you own all have a heavily influencing effect. These are all real world things with substance.

Displaying High Value comes after Money and Material Wealth, because Displays of High Value are the *style* to Money's *substance*. You can fake having High Value by acting all confident and cocky, but you can't fake the ability to actually pay the bills and put food on the table. There's just something about watching your car being repossessed that trumps you pretending everything is fine.

Having said that, Displays of High Value are what most people go on for determining social dominance and sexual value, and you can Build

104

Relationship Comfort all you like, but others discount it unless you're Displaying High Value first.

Building Relationship Comfort trumps your Personality and Preferences, because ultimately most people are self-interested. They want to be assured they will get their needs meet before attending to someone else's. Put another way, people want to build a positive relationship first before really determining to be interested in you in particular. For a couple of weeks you might just be a coffee barista to me, but after that I might learn your name is Janet and you're in college doing a Master's Degree.

High-Energy Sex comes last. Before someone wants to jump into a serious relationship and/or bed with you, typically you've had to pass all five hurdles before reaching the bedroom. Note that it can happen very quickly if someone has all the goodies lined up already, or it can take some time, but there's not much getting around having to get five green lights before it all comes together.

Stopping Red Gets the Quickest Gains

As you begin the process of creating your Mindful Attraction Plan, know that stopping all the Red issues as quickly as you can is going to give you the biggest, easiest and fastest energy gains. Do this no matter where it falls in the Order of Operations I just laid out.

The Reds are as serious as a hole in the bottom of a boat. It just doesn't matter what they are serving for lunch on B-Deck... if you have major trouble down below you have to fix it right now.

The good news is that the Reds are usually easily fixable, cost next to nothing to fix and you can handle them all within a week or two by changing your actions. The Reds are all things you're actively screwing up for yourself, all you have to do is stop doing them.

Doing nothing more than shutting off all the energy drains can have rather dramatic results. If you manage to stop a lot of Reds, there can be a major boost to your overall energy levels. Friends and family can be stunned into disbelief at first and will watch you keenly to see if you can hold steady on your changes.

If you do nothing else in the first month of running your MAP, get the Reds under control and hold steady. Obviously if it's an addiction you're getting under control, that can take some time, but it's unquestionably important to do with a high priority.

Maintain Your Current Greens

If you're doing something right, keep it up. It's all good.

Triage Your Yellows

I can't spin this one much, other than to say this is the hard part, but it's all going to be worth it.

Because this is just a book as opposed to a 1:1 coaching session, you're going to have to figure out for yourself the order you're going to fix the Yellows in. The long-term goal is to fix all the Yellow issues, giving general priority to the Yellows higher up the Order of Operations. If something is going to be an easy fix though, just do it.

Fixing all the Yellows might very well take a couple of *years*. If you're seriously overweight, well that's going to take time. If you're deep in debt, that will take time too. These are all long-term structural issues you need to fix. Be patient and stick with it.

As You Can, Turn On the Greens

While you work on the Yellows, keep an eye on the Greens you don't have turned on. As you get more of the Yellows under control, you'll find that some of the Greens all but self-resolve with minimal effort.

There's Too Much to Do All At Once

There's no question that the MAP is like the mother of all to-do lists. It's a long-term project for you to get your life under control and have it be as high-energy as you can. Don't sweat it, just start. It can start out as a jumbled mess, but like doing a jigsaw puzzle, all it takes is patience and the more you complete the puzzle, the easier it gets to fill in what's left to do.

With each little success along the way, you'll feel better and gain momentum to fix other areas of your life.

The Yellow Adaptation Problem

This one really applies to the Yellows. The more you work on a particular Yellow, the harder it can become to make progress on it.

For example if you're trying to lose weight and need to lose sixty pounds, the first forty pounds can just fall off you, but then the next five pounds take forever. Often you'll find you're stuck fifteen pounds from your goal and nothing seems to make any difference. It's as if you hit a wall.

The temptation here is to double up on your effort and try even harder to bash your way through the last fifteen pounds. Unfortunately that's not going to work because your body has adapted to the exercise and has stalled out and now you're feeling negative emotions about losing weight, which doesn't help at all.

The solution is to simply hold steady on maintenance exercise, give up on the weight loss and focus on a different Yellow completely. If you stall on weight loss, it is what it is. Now try making more money instead, or figuring out if double binds or covert contracts have you caught. Anything is better than fixating on the weight issue. If you make it a sole focus of your life and hurl huge amounts of negative emotion and energy at the problem, it will only intensify.

107

Once you've reached a plateau on your other Yellows, then you can double back and have another go at the weight loss. With more energy and the problem feeling fresher, you'll make more progress. You don't have to win every area all in one single step.

When looked at together, the two problems of There's Too Much To Do At Once and The Adaptation Problem, seem more like a mutual solution circle. One fixes the other. As always, just get active and do something it's always better than doing nothing.

Red = Draining = Stop It

Yellow = Stagnant = Fix It

Green = Flowing = Do It

Chapter 10 – The Elephant in the Room

Lies, Damn Lies and Elephants

I've now spent thousands of hours coaching people and I only have one thing to say.

Y'all are liars.

Essentially everyone with a critical energy or relationship issue tells me a huge raft of information when I start coaching them. I ask a lot of questions on intake. I mean I ask a. Lot. Of. Questions. About. Everything.

I love discovering how a person's life all fits together and where I can find a way to make it even better. I need to know everything and usually it all goes great, but it sometimes blows up, leaving me wondering why it all went wrong.

Then they tell me about the Elephant in the Room.

"Oh yeah, I cheated on my wife four years ago and that's when everything changed."

"Oh yeah, that's when my mother died and she refused to come with me to her funeral."

"Oh yeah, I drink until I black out."

"Oh yeah, the first time I had sex I was raped."

"Oh yeah, she told me she kissed a guy on New Year's Eve."

"Oh yeah, we were married to other people when we started seeing each other."

So...

I know you just went through that set of chapters and probably jotted down a list of Red, Yellow and Green things to do and think about. However, your Elephant in the Room, that's the thing you're thinking about right now, that thing that if I was sitting opposite you, you'd *really* rather not mention...

...that's your Elephant in the Room.

Think of it as a giant Red issue you're spending your whole life working around. Without getting that under control, you're only going to make moderate progress on your life plan.

"Being functional means having a lot of Greens and not many Reds or Yellows. The Elephant in the Room is a giant Red area."

PART TWO
Fixing The Problem

Being lonely, broke, unhappy, overweight, in a bad relationship, or undersexed are all major life problems.

The solution is to see these individual problems, not as individual problems, but as part of a larger set of energy. As you change your overall energy, the individual problems all more easily resolve.

Your overall energy level, sexual attractiveness and ability to attract success all link together in a positive feedback cycle. As one area improves, they all get better.

However, there is usually an area of your life that is *your major problem* that Drains and Stagnates your entire life. This critical area is very resistant to switching energy sets and requires a conscious and planned strategy to unseat it. Usually every other area of your life needs to be Flowing before this critical area responds to the change in energy set.

Once it changes though, it's an amazing breakthrough.

In addition, *it's always a relationship of some kind.* You're going to have a deep connection to your major problem, but you can only change you. You cannot change them, only influence them with your changes.

"The meeting of two personalities is like the contact of two chemical substances; if there is any reaction, both are transformed."

– Carl Jung

Chapter 11 – Energy Vampires and Victims

My Relationship is Perfect Except For...

...the thing where the Vampire drains all your life energy and leaves you a shattered wreck.

Often the Elephant in the Room is the situation where one-half of the couple has a critical problem area in their life and their spouse has to carry the marriage. It's also common that both of them have become conditioned to the situation and see it as an okay marriage, or a good marriage with just one little trouble spot.

I get a lot of mail from husbands who simply gush about the wonders of their wives, except for the sexless nature of their relationship for several years. I get a lot of mail from wives saying they have a happy marriage and are married to a great guy, except he's been unemployed for three years and stopped looking for work two years ago.

Half the battle is trying to define what a normal functional relationship looks like, so the Elephant in the Room comes into clearer focus.

Normal Functional Relationship

By Functional, I mean that if you leave your partner to their own devices, they would be able to support themselves in the activities of daily living. They would be capable of getting up in the morning, making breakfast, doing their personal hygiene, driving a car to work, being productive at work, coming home and cooking dinner. They could balance a checkbook, get to a doctor's appointment, parent a kid, shop for groceries and all the usual everyday things.

Being Functional means being a standard issue adult. It means being a self-supporting person who can handle themselves without constantly needing rescue.

Being Functional means being a person who isn't Batshit Crazy and constantly rampaging about something.

Being Functional means not being constantly sick, ill, injured or addicted through your own folly.

Being Functional also includes being able to have a normal sexual experience with your partner on a regular basis. Penis works as per the manual. Vagina doesn't growl and show its teeth.

Put in terms of this book, being Functional means having a lot of Greens and not very many Red's or Yellows to worry about.

However, if one-half of the couple is *Less*-Functional, their partner has to pick up the slack and be *More*-Functional. If the Less-Functional partner is unemployed and plays video games all day, that means the other partner needs to become More-Functional and pick up overtime hours or a second job.

If the Less-Functional partner is an alcoholic and prone to random property destruction and fist fights in the pub, their More-Functional partner will have to clean up the mess and deal with a partner locked in the police cells for a day here and there.

 As you might guess, that's fine for short bursts, but not sustainable on a permanent basis.

Short Term Crisis

Life doesn't always go according to plan. When this sort of thing happens, you just pick up the slack. That's why you got married in the first place isn't it? It's the buddy system. You go down and your buddy pulls you up, your buddy goes down you pull him or her up. Win-Win.

If a husband is doing great at work, but suddenly they downsize his entire department, it's a terrible shock and without his income, he feels Less-Functional. For a while, it's fine that his wife picks up extra shifts at her job and becomes More-Functional.

The next year some idiot sideswipes her car and she breaks her leg in two places. Now she's the Less-Functional one. Therefore, he becomes the More-Functional one, picks up more of the chores around the house and drives her to work each morning while she recovers from the accident.

Those little scenarios work out fine because they are short-term conditions that resolve eventually. A couple months after the downsizing, he finds a new job and she stops picking up extra shifts. Six weeks after her accident, she's out of the cast and everything is back to normal. They restore the natural relationship balance.

Long Term Crisis

The buddy system works great for a short-term crisis, but it starts to backfire in a long-term crisis as one partner ends up chronically supporting the other one. Instead of it simply being a Less-Functional and More-Functional pairing, it turns into a Vampire and Victim couple.

In the case of the downsized husband, the wife automatically picked up extra shifts to cover his lost income. The risk is that when she covers the lost income, he essentially refuses to find his way back into the workforce and checks out into an early retirement of beer and Xbox. If that continues for very long at all, the husband has won an easy lifestyle at the wife's expense. The husband has become the Vampire and the wife the Victim.

Or, let's say the wife with the broken leg finally gets her cast off, but then refuses to resume any of the additional chores the husband took on to let her rest and recover. If the husband simply continues with all the chores, the wife just got house cleaning services forever at his expense. The wife is now the Vampire and the husband the Victim.

What worked so well in the short-term crisis, turns out to be what *creates* the long-term crisis. The Victim *enables* the Vampire to be the Vampire. Once you've started enabling your partner to become an energy Vampire, it's always a major effort to get them to return to normal functioning. They nearly always fight you trying to change things, because when you turned yourself into their Victim, they saw it as a Display of Low Value.

Your Display of Low Value means they perceive themselves as being the more attractive half of the couple and therefore feel entitled to demand you continuously earn the right to stay in a relationship with them. Thus, you must continue to enable and serve them, or face, in their mind, justifiable punishment or dumping. They demand that must spend your energy on them, or else.

This explains why living with a Vampire... *sucks.*

Golden Handcuffs

If you have an extremely demanding profession, or toxic workplace, your Vampire may be your job.

All jobs have positives and negatives. The negative for going to work is that you expend a certain amount of energy each day and end up feeling physically and mentally tired. The positive is that you are paid energy in the form of money for working. The amount of energy you are paid is usually greater than the energy you spent working, so having a job is a net gain for your overall energy levels.

However, some jobs are very demanding on your time and mental energy and don't pay a sufficient amount to really warrant the experience of actually showing up to work, unless you happen to really need the money and are trapped there. In cases like these, the job actually is a net energy loss where you're the Victim and the workplace is the Vampire.

Most workplaces aren't intentionally cruel, but some work environments are keenly aware of just how much an employee is trapped into their job, and they actively target them for greater productivity output. Put another way, if they know you're wearing a pair of golden handcuffs, you're going to get some really crappy assignments to handle.

It also doesn't matter whether the golden handcuffs are a $500,000 salary or a minimum wage job. If they know they have you trapped at their mercy, you're at a serious disadvantage. If you've ever tried to talk to a bad employer who thinks they have you by the wallet, you'll have likely experienced being told something between, *"Sorry we can't help you."* and *"If you don't like it you can leave."*

Then you get another crappy assignment just so you understand who is boss.

The Needs of the Many, Outweigh the Needs of You

Vampires can peer pressure you into being a Victim.

Most social groups, whether it is a circle of friends, club, church, band, political organization, scouts or anything else, are benign. You give your time and energy to the group, getting back positive energy through fun and socializing. It's all good. Everyone loves to be included in a group of people.

Unfortunately, some groups get increasingly concerned about getting your energy spent on the group's activities, which always seem to benefit *the group's leadership* subtly. If you could just give a little more of your time, a little more of your effort, a little more of your money, that would be a good thing. Right?

Now for the most part, there's usually some sort of shakedown for energy with every group at least occasionally. Sell these cookies, buy the yearbook, come work the popcorn stand at the fair for us. That's all normal and expected. It's not abusive to ask you to support something that is giving a clear benefit to you or your family.

However, when that shakedown stops being a polite request and starts becoming a direct demand, with negative consequences for failing to comply, that can start heading into very toxic waters. When you start not wanting to comply with the directives of the group, but do so anyway for fear of social sanction, you're essentially being peer pressured into something you don't want to do.

You don't have to be a teenager to face peer pressure. Watch this...

"Everyone else has given $1000 dollars. How much can we expect your gift to be?"

If you automatically thought $1000, that's because peer pressure works.

Peer pressure works via a number of negative communication methods. Some are overt with angry demands and outright threats, some are rather covert with implied guilt and shaming. Ultimately, though, everything comes back to one core message – that the needs of the group are more important than you are. The group would rather see you quit, than have you stay and not be compliant.

The other wrinkle is that it's often not really meeting the needs of the group that are the true demands. The true demands are meeting the needs of the group's leadership. Whether those needs are ego, income or other, doesn't really matter that much.

Anyway, we still need that $1000 from you. *It's for the children.*

"If you get yourself into a bad place in your life, that's when the Vampires show up to help you."

Best Vampire Forever!

Sometimes the Vampire is a toxic friendship.

The classic way a friendship turns toxic, is when the best friend attempts to demand the friendship become the *de facto* primary relationship. They demand the time, attention and loyalty the true primary partner deserves for themselves.

Over the thousands of people I've coached, I've seen a typical pattern of relationship destruction from best friends. The female best friend of the wife tends to drag her away from her husband in order to act as a cohort and/or cover story for seeking fun and excitement and eventually other men. These girls' nights out almost always spark jealousy and fear in the husband, while the wife and best friend accuse him of being paranoid and controlling.

The male best friend of the husband more typically seeks to insert himself in the mix to gain opportunities to isolate with the wife. He will typically seek to trump the husband by displaying greater skills, putting down the husband in front of the wife and being sexually provocative toward the wife as soon as the husband's back is turned.

To be sure, having same sex friends is great, but when they seek to trump the primary relationship, they quickly become toxic and must stop.

Friendly Vampires

There are situations where some people become Vampires by true accident, or due to extreme young or old age.

Having a baby or toddler in the house is like having a tiny Vampire that poops. They absolutely aren't trying to ruin your day, but no one can deny that babies suck up a huge amount of your energy keeping up with them. Yes, they are wonderful little bundles with smiles that melt your heart, but truthfully, you give them far more energy than they give you.

That's totally fine though, you expect it to be that way... *but you only tolerate it because it doesn't last forever.* It's a short-term crisis.

Elderly parents moving in with you can also act as friendly Vampires. Yes, it's fine at first, but eventually as they age, it can get harder and harder to cope with their needs. You can have the patience of a saint, but after several years of providing difficult care, the caregiver can be exhausted beyond all reason.

The same sort of thing can happen with genuinely injured or ill spouses. Everyone tends to focus on the needs of the cancer stricken spouse and support them, far fewer focus on the needs of the supporting spouse. Toward the end of things, even a multi-decade sweet and happy marriage can slowly turn into a Vampire and Victim arrangement.

No one wants to be a bad parent, child or spouse. As a result, caregivers tend to err on the side of allowing them to go to the limits of physical endurance, before finally breaking down and asking for help. Love is a wonderful thing, but sometimes it just isn't enough coming from only one or two people.

Please seek outside help before you reach a breaking point.

Talking Fails and You Must Take Action

Assuming you have a Vampire Draining you constantly, the question is what to do about it.

A classic mistake to make is when the Victim believes the real solution is that the Vampire just magically realizes they are acting poorly and decides to change for the better. Therefore, the Victim asks the Vampire repeatedly to stop Draining them in varying degrees of nagging, begging, complaining and crying.

Unfortunately, the Victim's tears nourish the Vampire.

The Vampire will never change as long as the Vampire believes the Victim won't let the relationship fail. As silly as it may sound, the Victim believes they need the Vampire and the Vampire knows it. The more the Victim talks to the Vampire about changing for the better, the more the Victim frames the Vampire as the powerful one in the relationship. Thus, the less likely the Vampire is to care about anything the Victim says.

After enough time, the Victim starts sounding like "The Boy Who Cried Wolf". The Vampire just gives up listening because there's no real danger of a wolf, divorce papers, resignation letter or just quitting the social group. It's all just an idle threat and no cause for concern. The Vampire is motivated to keep the current arrangement because it's working perfectly well for them.

You can't talk your way out of being a Vampire's Victim, you have to take action and stop them Draining you. Just think of them as a huge Red area of your life Draining you constantly. You know you have to stop them from doing that.

Red — Just Stop the Vampire?

It's always tempting to just have a screaming fit and divorce your spouse, quit your job or tell your toxic social group to go take a hike.

However, you probably need them more than they need you right now. If you blow it all up today, things will be worse. *They are your Vampire because you need them.*

"The Victim role is just as negative as the Vampire role."

Fake Green — The Vampire is Fine?

Well you could pretend everything is just fine, but you're probably just so weak from the Vampire Draining you that you don't want to fight them.

The longer you tolerate a Vampire the harder it is to break free. The other word for "pretending" is "denial". Don't keep tolerating the intolerable.

Yellow — Resolve the Vampire Situation

The true solution is to get yourself into the position where you don't need the Vampire anymore.

The trouble is that the Vampire is the sole supplier of what you need, so they have a monopoly over you and set the price where they like. You're always going to need whatever it is that they give you, so you have no other option other than to put yourself in the position where you have the ability to seek other supplies of what you need. It may take some time to get yourself in a place where you can do that, but once there, you can cause the situation to resolve in your favor.

If your Vampire is a social group's leadership, either you become capable of being the leader, or you find an alternate group you can join.

If your Vampire is your employer or job, you become capable of finding a better employer or job to hire you.

If your Vampire is your primary partner, you become capable of easily replacing them with another person of equal or better hotness.

If your Vampire is your best friend, you become capable of finding a new best friend.

As you become capable of finding a new supplier of what the Vampire gives you, very often the Vampire suddenly starts acting right, without having any kind of dramatic confrontation. They just sense your whole energy pattern shifting to Displaying High Value and they start valuing you more highly.

Sometimes though, you will have to demand either they stop being a Vampire, or the agreement you have together will end. In the next chapters, I'll talk about how to manage that confrontation over seven clear phases of action. It's hardball, but works by slowing the rush to ending the agreement down to a "bullet-time" slow-motion confrontation, giving the Vampire time to react to your attempts to positively resolve things.

Chapter 12 – Dealing With Your Energy Vampire

Reframing to a Positive Approach

You've probably already tried the negative energy approach where you complained, nagged, begging and got angry at your energy Vampire for not fixing their problem. I understand how it's tempting, but it's just layer after layer of negative energy, focusing on a problem.

Here's the triple whammy of negative energy...

(1) Your strong negative feelings.
(2) Framing the Vampire as the only one who can change things.
(3) Focusing all your energy on the problem.

Here's what that sounds like...

"I'm so angry that you haven't stopped drinking when I have begged you over and over to stop drinking, and I HATE that you don't listen to me, or seem to care about our family. I cannot take any more of your drinking and I'm miserable in this marriage."

I can understand that emotional state, but all that negativity just locks the situation into place. There's no hope for a positive resolution expressed in there. The complainer wants the situation to become more positive, but they unleash an avalanche of negativity. Feelings and energy are infectious; negativity begets more negativity. The complaining makes the situation worse.

I know you've already tried that and failed, so you have nothing to lose by trying a positive approach...

(1) Your strong positive feelings.
(2) Framing yourself as the one in control of you.
(3) Focus all your energy on a positive future that they can't stop from happening.

Here's what a positive approach sounds like...

"I've decided that I'm going to have a happy and positive relationship. To do that, I need to be a happy and functional person myself and I'm going to work on that from now on. I also know I need to be with a happy and functional person, because any positive relationship needs a win-win balance. I would very much like that person to be you, but if you can't be that person, I know I'll find someone else who can be. I've decided to be happy no matter what; your only choice is whether or not you'll be happy."

Having heard that, can you *feel* the difference between the two statements? Try not to think about it and rationalize, just imagine how you would *feel* hearing both of those messages. I say "feel" rather than "think", because people don't make serious behavioral choices based on critical thinking skills very often, they do it based on their feelings.

You're trying to move from a negative energy set of interactions, to a positive energy set of interactions, so you can only get there by using positive methods. Anything else just keeps you locked in negativity.

You Aren't Punishing the Vampire

It's also worth noting now that you don't want to punish the Vampire, or even end up breaking your relationship with the Vampire off. All you want is for the Vampire to stop treating you terribly and have a normal functional relationship together. You aren't going to be using nasty tricks or cruelty either. You're just getting to a place where the reality of the situation is that you no longer need to tolerate poor treatment.

If the problem is an employer thing, what you want is a good work environment.

If the problem is your primary partner, what you want is a good family life.

If the problem is a social group, what you want is a good social group.

Vampires are always relationships of some kind and if they end up failing, it's because they preferred treating you badly so much, they would rather end the relationship than treat you well.

It's worth noting that the Vampire will always claim you are punishing them, or say you're a bad person when you start pushing things toward a proper relationship. Don't fall for them complaining, it's just them wanting you to keep being a Victim.

The Four Outcome Matrix

There are four different possible outcomes a relationship can reach when pushed toward the Resolution Point. It's worth talking about what those outcomes are to clarify why you need to push things toward a resolution rather than simply wait things out.

One – Tolerance. With Tolerance, essentially nothing changes. This is where rather than doing anything, you simply continue to put up with whatever nasty stuff is happening and don't try to rock the boat about it. This is the default outcome of the four. If you do nothing, your Vampire just keeps Draining you forever. Nothing changes apart from different degrees of daily pain and suffering.

Two – Cheating. With Cheating, you simply give up on trying to get what you need from the relationship directly and somehow break the rules to get what you want anyway, without breaking the relationship with the Vampire. So if you're in a terrible job, you stay in the terrible job, but you become a bad employee just doing the bare minimum to stay employed, or you start stealing things from the company, or giving friends and family extremely good and unapproved discounts.

If it's your primary relationship, you end up going outside the relationship to look for love, sex or even income. He gets a mistress, she spends three hours a day chatting with an old boyfriend on Facebook, there's a secret credit card account.

In a social group, you start making excuses to avoid fully participating and begin church hopping, or somehow miss picking up the box of chocolate bars to sell for the fundraiser, or you're going online and writing things against the group's interest on your social media.

Note that sometimes you're even encouraged by the Vampire to break the rules to keep the relationship intact. Sometimes wives actually tell husbands *"It's okay if you get a girlfriend."* However, that's also a very clear statement that she only values her husband for non-sexual reasons.

Three – End It. One possible outcome is that the Victim just gives up trying to change things and ends the relationship. They quit their job. They file for divorce or wash their hands of the social group.

Sometimes this is done in a moment of rage where they snap, but also often there is a Plan B job / affair partner / group already lined up to make as quick a transition as possible from the old relationships to the new one. The best version of this allows time to get to a much higher quality relationship after the end of the current one. Though there is always the risk of "out of the frying pan, into the fire".

Four – Positive Resolution. This is where you do the hard work of the MAP and actually manage to get your relationship to change for the better. Your job gets more resources and less stress, your primary relationship becomes loving and sexual, you end up leading your social group and making positive changes.

This is the hardest outcome to reach, but it's usually the best one. As a caveat though, even with the MAP I can't promise that you'll end up with everything you wanted in an Outcome Four ending. You can't control what the other side of the relationship does, only influence them the way you want them to go. All I'm promising is that the relationship will resolve somehow and you can get unstuck from your Vampire.

"Feelings and energy are infectious. Negativity begets more negativity. Your complaining can make the situation worse."

Heading Toward the Resolution Point

The Resolution Point is where the relationship makes a clear move toward one of the four outcomes. It could happen in a five-minute conversation, or it could happen gradually over a couple weeks, but it's usually a fairly well defined time where you can look back and see that everything came into its new focus.

The next chapter is going to cover the systematic process of bringing the relationship toward its resolution point, but for now I want to talk about what happens at the Resolution Point.

The Victim sees the Four Outcomes looking like this...

(1) Tolerance = I get taken advantage of.
(2) Cheating = I never get what I want, so I'm forced to break the rules.
(3) End It = I'll never get what I want, so I'm leaving to find a new relationship.
(4) Positive Resolution = I'll get a positive relationship.

The Vampire sees it like this...

(1) Tolerance = I am pampered.
(2) Cheating = I'll get what I want, but they will betray me.
(3) End It = I'll be dumped and not get what I want.
(4) Positive Resolution = I'll have to behave better, but I'll be treated fairly.

The entire goal of pushing toward the Resolution Point is to remove the Victim's requirement that they Tolerate the Vampire. Once they can get what the Vampire gives them from somewhere else, they can leverage that to remove the Tolerance outcome from the Matrix.

In addition, the Victim can take the moral high ground and refuse to decide for the Cheating outcome, which makes the Four Outcome Matrix suddenly look like this...

The Victim sees...

(1) ~~Tolerance = I get taken advantage of.~~
(2) ~~Cheating = I never get what I want, so I'm forced to break the rules.~~
(3) End It = I'll never get what I want, so I'm leaving to find a new relationship.
(4) Positive Resolution = I'll get a positive relationship.

The Vampire sees it like this...

(1) ~~Tolerance = I am pampered.~~
(2) ~~Cheating = I'll get what I want, but they will betray me.~~
(3) End It = I'll be dumped and not get what I want.
(4) Positive Resolution = I'll have to behave better, but I'll be treated fairly.

For the Victim, BOTH available outcomes are winning outcomes. They would obviously prefer not to have the relationship fail, but either way it plays out, they will end up with the sort of relationship they want to have.

For the Vampire, one option ends up with them dumped and unwanted and one option ends up being an acceptable and reasonable compromise. Usually because they want to have their *own needs* met, they'll choose the Positive Resolution outcome and start acting right. If they choose the other option, it means they don't really love the Victim and nothing the Victim does will ever change that.

It's also worth saying that the Vampire will often ultimately find that they much prefer being with someone with high enough value to insist on Option 3 or 4. However, they won't feel that way until the Victim stands up for themselves.

"When one side of a relationship is in a negative energy state, the other side is also in a negative energy state."

Why You Have No Choice

When one side of a relationship is in a negative energy state, the other side of the relationship is likely also in a negative energy state. The emotions on each side are likely different though. While you may be depressed about things, they may be bored and checked out. You may be angry with them, but they feel contempt for you. You feel exhausted and confused, while they feel lonely and sad.

Therefore, while you might not be feeling compelled to push the situation toward the Resolution Point... *they might be*.

If they push for resolution, there's not always going to be a flashing neon sign that tells you they are considering the Cheating or End It outcomes right now, or are even already in the Cheating outcome. They aren't going to tell you they are Cheating, because cheating by definition means not playing fair. Your first warning of the End It outcome might happen when your boss calls you into her office at 4:15pm on Friday. Another warning could be when your partner hands you divorce papers to sign.

The whole point is that the Vampire doesn't really care what happens to the Victim, it's all about the Vampire. This means you have no choice other than to make yourself the best option possible for the Vampire, head to the Resolution Point and control the frame when you by getting there *first*.

Critical Caveats

As an important aside, there are things that are just so out of line that working patiently toward the Resolution Point isn't the best idea. You have to cut to the chase and lay it all on the line from the get go.

Things like domestic violence, an employer asking you to perform illegal acts, discovering your primary partner is having an affair, serious misuse of funds, genuine levels of Batshit Crazy in a primary partner, these are all things that require a strong and immediate response. You can't simply try to think positive thoughts and work through it. You need outside help.

I'm only saying "resolution" here. I can't 100% promise your Vampire will start behaving well and treating you right. They will always have some sort of period where they push back on your changes to test you and in the short term, their behavior may get worse. Ultimately though, you can't make them do anything, you can only influence them.

However, I can promise if you apply yourself to running your MAP, that you will have a happier, more positive life. The Vampire may not be welcome though.

The next chapter covers how to move toward Resolution Point in the best possible way.

Chapter 13 – The Mindful Attraction Plan

You Planned to be Where You Are Now

Up until this part of the book, I've been telling you about an endless pile of individual thought points. You've probably found yourself thinking, *"I knew that already"* repeatedly on a number of points. I'm sure you already knew that you needed to exercise, or have a rainy day fund, or act attractively and take time for yourself. Everyone knows those things already, it's doing them that is hard. Everything has been building to this point where I pull the camera back and show you the big picture of the forest you've been lost in.

All those little things you know you should be doing matter, because each one has a small influence on every other positive or negative factor in your life. Everything you do ties together into a coherent pattern. Right now, it's probably a coherent negative pattern and you want to change it to a positive one.

A coherent positive pattern is going to be very orderly, calm, relaxed, fun and enjoyable.

A coherent negative pattern is going to be chaotic, stressful, endlessly problematic, unhappy and miserable.

Whether you're having a coherent positive or negative energy lifestyle, you have to understand that it's something you've spent a lot of effort methodically planning and building. Yes, I realize bad things happened to you along the way, but after several decades of being alive, if you were in an unhappy lifestyle, wouldn't it be fair to say you had at least some influence over getting yourself to where you are?

Assume you spent four years in college, partying, getting barely passing grades, for a degree major with poor employment prospects and finish with $60,000 in loans. If you then find the only place that's willing to hire

132

you is a retail outlet and you're broke trying to make the loan payments, that would be something you actively planned to happen.

The Victim attracts the Vampire. When you're in a low-energy state, that's when the Vampires come into your life. The Vampire always has something you need and you willingly pay the price out of desperation. Thus the solution to removing a Vampire, always requires you to find a way to become less needy and have higher energy.

It's time to pull the camera back so you can see the big picture and the way out of this mess. It's going to take some time, but you can get there.

Be Mindful

Being mindful is about becoming self-aware in the moment and understanding the causality of your actions.

You need to experience your feelings not just as feelings, but become aware that you are experiencing those feelings as a response to reality. Your feelings are not the external reality itself. Your feelings are something happening inside you based on neurochemicals and hormones. If you can learn to control your *expression* of your feelings, you can change how other people respond to you. For example if you are about to be bullied it's natural to feel fearful. If you express fear, the bullying happens, but if you express calm and amused confidence, often the bullying never occurs. Thus, your *expressed* emotional state was the only thing that changed the outcome of the interaction.

The feelings that you express into the world are infectious to others. Your mindful expression of a positive and productive attitude when problem solving is far more likely to get the results you want than negativity is.

Whether you want them to be or not, your actions are the true message you send to others. You may verbally tell someone you are unhappy with them, but if you then give them something nice or perform an act of service, you're actually expressing that you're willing to do what they want even if you don't want to. That's a message of weakness and a display of low value.

133

In addition, if you allow your feelings to dominate your decision-making, your entire frame of reference becomes extremely short term. It's usually more tempting to do something pleasurable now, as opposed to delay gratification to a more enjoyable period in the future. Given choices between an expensive vacation and retirement planning, if you fall prey to your desire for immediate enjoyment, the expensive vacation wins out. The inability to delay gratification leads to the biggest personal downfalls.

Being mindful is an easy to do, but hard to master sort of thing. Be present in the moment, consider the consequences of your actions, then act.

You Can't Change Them

You have to give up the idea that you can directly change other people to do what you want them to. Other people are going to do whatever it is they want to do, based on their own self-interest and motivations. You asking them to change will do nothing.

All you can do is change yourself and be a different factor in other people's lives, and have them react differently to you. You being a lousy, unattractive jerk will get you treated one way. You being confident, attractive and playful will get you treated another way.

Even then, when you change it's only going to be an influence on their behavior. There are no magic bullets.

"You have to give up the idea that you can directly change other people to do what you want them to. All you can do is change yourself and have them react differently to you."

Just 0.1% Better Today

There's often a sense that fixing your life is a huge and impossible task. Rather than fixate on everything your life is not, acknowledge that there's a long way to go and take one day at a time.

When you wake up in the morning, what's one thing you could do to make your life just a tiny bit better? Even just 0.1% better is fine. I know 0.1% sounds like hardly anything, but after a while, it really starts adding up.

If you stick with it, after a year your life would be at least 36.5% better. *That's huge.*

After ten years, your life would be 365% better than it is now. What would that look like?

It's possible, but only if you don't get fixated on trying to improve the same area of your life over and over.

The Mindful Attraction Plan

The Mindful Attraction Plan is a seven-phase process to change you for the better, in order to leverage your critical issue to resolve the way you want it to. Most threats of ending relationships in hope of change, fail because of extremely poor timing. The MAP covers the pacing of the escalation toward the Resolution Point.

Most serious attempts to change things happen in the heat of the moment, which is typically a negative emotion blowout and ineffective. The MAP keeps things calm and steady in the hope that the Vampire starts acting like a reasonable person and the relationship can start turning positive.

The next seven chapters will discuss each phase in detail, but here's the quick summary...

Phase One – This is when you're in a very low-energy state and utterly dependent on your Vampire. The goal here is to get all your Red areas under control.

Phase Two – You're at a place where things are no longer terrible and there's a more even balance between you and your Vampire. You still can't break free of them yet, though. Your goal is to work on your Yellow areas.

Phase Three – Things are getting better and you're working on improving the Greens. You've gotten to the point where you don't need your Vampire quite so much. You verbally request that the Vampire treat you better.

Phase Four – If the verbal requests in Phase Three fail, you can move to Phase Four and give clear demonstrations of unhappiness with the relationship by your actions. You're displaying the willingness to end the relationship if the Vampire doesn't start to act right. This is a very short phase.

Phase Five – If Phase Four fails, you begin to withdraw your support from the Vampire and let natural consequences of that lack of support manifest. You begin getting your ducks in a row for potential exit from the relationship.

Phase Six – An Option A or B ultimatum is given to the Vampire. Option A means the Vampire complies with your demands. Option B means the relationship is ended.

Phase Seven – You transition to a life without a Vampire.

"A positive energy pattern is orderly, calm, relaxed, fun and enjoyable, while a negative energy pattern is stressful, problematic, unhappy and miserable."

136

The Resolution Point is Random

Because you can't control other people, there's no way of knowing when you will hit the Resolution Point.

If you're extremely lucky, the Resolution Point might be as you transition from Phase One to Phase Two. Maybe all it takes for your employer to stop riding you as hard is getting a few Red areas under control. Maybe as soon as you find work, stop drinking and stop being so grumpy, your partner wants to restart your sex life.

Often the Resolution Point comes in Phase Three with barely a hint of drama or conflict. You're suddenly just that much better of a person and they want you and need you, so they start treating you right. They can start qualifying themselves to you by trying to please you, rather than demand you please them. In Phase Three, you become the one that could be the Vampire, so rather than fight you, they just start to comply with you peacefully.

Phase Four is when you have to shock them, because some people simply don't admit the reality until they really see you willing to take action.

In Phase Five, you start to take back what the Vampire wants from you and that can trigger the Resolution Point.

If they absolutely refuse to make changes, Phase Six forces the Resolution Point on them for a final ultimatum.

Outcome Independence

You can't fixate on your current relationship turning out great as a condition of the MAP.

In the last chapter, we talked about the MAP pushing things to one of two positive outcomes for you. They started treating you better and made it a proper relationship, or you moved on to find a new relationship where you were treated the way you want to be treated.

The temptation is that you become fixated on the ending where they love you back and not the one where you find a new life for yourself. If they sense you're still emotionally fixated on them, they know they're still in the driver's seat as the Vampire. They'll see your loyalty as a weakness.

You have to be willing to push it all the way or they will call your bluff. You simply won't know how far you have to push things to reach the point where they stop treating you poorly and start acting right.

They will *always* call your bluff.

Vampires and Victims Equally to Blame

The Victim role is just as negative as the Vampire role.

Negative energy draws negative energy. It's like the thing where a woman has an abusive boyfriend, leaves him, finds a new abusive boyfriend, leaves that boyfriend and finds... another abusive boyfriend.

We all attract and co-create things into our life all the time. If you're in a bad marriage, a funky social group or a crazy company, you're there because you attracted it into your life and once it was apparent what was going on, you encouraged it to take over by not putting up enough of a fight. In part, it's your fault too.

Don't misunderstand this point, horrible bad luck can happen in anyone's life at any time. I think having a positive energy does provide *some* positive overall luck and protection, but consider it magic bubble wrap as opposed to magical seatbelts, bulletproof vests and a cancer vaccine.

Beyond that though, the major structural things in your life aren't random. You co-create them.

Trust the Process

What I can say is this: I've now seen thousands of people run this plan and have it work. If you get yourself into a higher energy state, good things will happen. I can't promise exactly what they are, but it will be better than where you are now.

Chapter 14 – Phase One

Definition

Phase One – This is when you're in a very low-energy state and utterly dependent on your Vampire. The goal here is to get all your Red areas under control.

Just Start

It doesn't matter what your starting point is, just start.

If possible, follow the Order of Operations in Chapter 9, but doing anything to get the ball rolling is better than doing nothing and staying where you are.

Anything. Seriously, do ANYTHING you can to get started. Just get a little win under your belt in any area. Even if it's nothing more than collecting all the trash in the house and taking it to the curb, it's a completed task and you'll feel better.

That being said, if you can only do one single thing to get going, the best thing to do at this point is to start an exercise routine. Physical fitness primes the energy and attraction pump on so many levels that you simply can't ignore physical fitness and body appearance.

Weakest Areas First

You get the biggest gains from your weakest areas.

Let's assume that you're a basically good guy with a great job pulling in say $100,000 a year as your primary selling point as a husband, but you're 50 pounds overweight, and that's your primary weakness. If you decide to do "more of what works", you might work an extra one or two hours a day and bust your ass up into a promotion and make $120,000 a year, but still be fat. The extra $20,000 is going to be nice, but it isn't really going to make your wife all that more excited sexually about you. It's a lot of effort for a slight improvement. But if you instead spent the extra time working out and getting in shape, now you're going to be a fit guy making $100,000 a year, and that's going to get much better results.

The opposite would hold true as well. Imagine now you're an in shape guy stuck in a crappy job making $24,000 a year. If you keep doing "more of what works", you might have to work crazy hard in the gym to get even more in shape, but still be making crappy money. It's a minor plus. However, if you hold the exercise steady and maintain what you have, and make a push to educate yourself and get a promotion up to a $40,000 job, that extra $16,000 a year is going to be huge.

Stealth Mode

If someone has demanded that you sort your life out, or risk a dumping or firing, my strong advice is that during Phase One you keep your mouth shut about you running your MAP.

If someone has been demanding you clean up your act and wants to hear a plan of action, then making them a minor presentation of *"This is what I'm doing to fix things."* is a reasonable thing to do.

Otherwise, you gain nothing at all by explaining your plan of action. Don't tell your employer that you plan to work like crazy for a year and then threaten to leave them unless they give you better treatment. Don't tell your primary partner you're miserable and they are horrible to you. Don't tell your social group they suck. Blowing it all up now will just get you fired, divorced or shunned and you'll lose something you need.

Also at some point, your Vampire will figure out you're actively planning to get yourself to the point where you could, if need be, replace them. That's going to be very threatening to the Vampire and they will always push back on that and demand you stop doing what you're doing. In Phase One that's going to be very damaging to you.

The good news is that in Phase One, the Vampire cares about you so little you barely register on their attention radar anyway. "Stealth Mode" amounts to not spilling your guts to them unprompted. If they ask you, just say you just felt like exercising, or doing whatever it is you're changing. It's hard to argue with you having a feeling.

They'll just assume you're in a short-term phase anyway. A month of the gym and you'll be back on the couch...

Be Agreeable and Polite

Don't pick stupid fights. Try to get along with your Vampire as best you can.

Stupid fights against a stronger opponent are negative energy events and make your situation worse. It's also good in that if you stop having direct conflict with your employer, partner or group, they actually relax a little and think the relationship has improved.

When they think the relationship has improved, they become less worried about forcing compliance tests on you and allow you more room to breathe and do what you need to do. As your primary goal in Phase One is to get to the gym and stop all your Red areas, having freedom to get that done is in your best interest.

You're in Phase One, so they have you over a barrel and you're going to end up doing what they want anyway. All you're doing by fighting them over individual points of direction is wasting your energy. Save your energy, complete their task for them and then do some more of your stuff.

Just bide your time.

"It doesn't matter what your starting point is, just start."

Chapter 15 – Phase Two

Definition

Phase Two – You're at a place where things are no longer terrible and there's a more even balance between you and your Vampire. You still can't break free of them yet though. Your Phase Two goal is to work on your Yellow areas.

Building Momentum

In Phase Two, you start feeling as things are starting to head in the right direction. By the time you have the majority of your Red areas handled, you should be starting to build a positive momentum. This is going to make your Vampire feel both good and a little uneasy.

On one hand, they've probably complained about you a lot regarding all of the things that were your Red areas. The Vampires always believe they are doing you a favor by letting you stick around and serve them. When you suddenly stop everything they've used to frame you as the problem in the relationship, they like it, but they also start to wonder exactly how far your momentum is going to carry you.

As far as the Vampire is concerned, if you could just stall out in Phase Two and not rock the boat too much, that would be great. Their quite reasonable fear is that if you keep the momentum going, you'll outgrow your need for the Vampire. Or worse, you'll take over the relationship and treat them like they treated you.

Sabotage!

Something to watch out for is your Vampire either purposely or unconsciously, trying to derail your progress of self-improvement running the MAP.

You're working out at the gym and starting to get real results. Thus explaining why they bake your favorite cookies and throw them in front of you every time they see you.

You've gotten your budget under control and everything is going great at work. For some reason though, your department gets to be the one who has to break in a new "best practice" for the rest of the company. It's a colossal pain in the ass and an additional task for no more pay. Your boss gets the credit if it all goes well and you get to take the fall if it doesn't.

You've been really pulling things together in your social group and making things happen. Then there's some kind of ugly rumor about you circling. A rumor about something you did not do, but can't prove you didn't. Your stock falls.

If they try to sabotage you, politely and calmly decline to be taken in. The trick is also to see it as you making progress and view it as a small victory. You can also playfully toss it back at them by verbalizing that they are in fact trying to sabotage you.

Start to Ask for What You Want

In Phase Two, you're pulling equal with your Vampire in terms of value, so it's fine to start making reasonable requests of them.

You aren't going to be demanding the big-ticket stuff, but you are going to be asking that some of the energy that you've been spending on them becomes more mutual. You're not so much demanding things, as simply asking for them. There's no threat in your tone, you're just simply asking for what you want.

If you get a yes, cool. If you get a no, say thank you and immediately transition to some other productive and positive activity. Don't just stand around and look upset. Always be mindful that you showing negative emotion about them saying "no" to you, frames them as the power in the relationship.

If you're seeking sex with your primary partner, don't leave it to the very last minute of the day. If you're already in bed when you initiate and suffer rejection, it's hard to seem unaffected if you're lying there horny and unable to fall asleep. If you ask earlier in the day and get a no, you can plan your evening accordingly.

Start to Say No

Saying no is the most powerful thing you can do in a relationship, but you have to say no to the right things.

If they are making reasonable requests of you, in a reasonable tone, it's reasonable that you say yes and help them. You want them to make reasonable requests in reasonable tones, so complying with these tasks is rewarding them for doing what you want them to do.

However, if they are clearly unreasonable requests or unreasonable tones, it's reasonable that you start saying "no" to what they are asking of you. Bear in mind that if it's your employer, or some professional relationship, even with unreasonable tones you may have to follow along quietly at this point.

There's an element of judgment call needed here obviously, but the general principle is if Phase One is a "yes to everything", Phase Two is "default setting is yes, but I will say no if I think it's needed".

"The major structural things in your life aren't random, you co-create them. Your own neediness traps you."

Nicer Treatment, Some Questions

Overall, in Phase Two you should be getting somewhat more pleasant treatment and questions about what exactly it is you're up to and what your intentions are.

Depending on how positively you think they will react to you running the MAP, you *may* wish to expose that you're reading the book and purposely working on things. Honestly though, you have no clear advantage in doing so if you think your relationship will need to go as far as Phase Four at this point. You don't want them to think Phase Four is "just something you read in a book", you want it to seem very real and scary that they botched the relationship.

Phase Two Can Be Long

Because Phase Two is about fixing up the Yellow areas as best you can, it might take a really long time before you really get things cooking and you transition into Phase Three.

Just be patient and grind it out.

It might take a year or longer in Phase Two to really get your momentum going. I know you're going to want instant results, but there's no way around doing the hard work of dealing with the Yellows.

On the bright side, even if your Vampire is still sucking the life out of you, fixing the Yellows is something you should have been doing for yourself anyway. It's not really that much harder than living a regular life.

Just keep up the effort.

Chapter 16 – Phase Three

Definition

Phase Three – Things are really getting better and you're working on improving the Greens. You've gotten to the point where you don't need your Vampire quite so much. You verbally request that the Vampire treat you better.

Rocking the Momentum

By now, it's becoming apparent to the Vampire that you have yourself in a pretty good position. They won't always let you know that though. In fact, they may verbally deny it to your face just to try to hold their own frame together where you're still the Victim and they're still the Vampire.

Just keep pushing ahead.

Dressed for Success

Often the trigger that flips you from Phase Two to Phase Three is a wardrobe upgrade, *on top of the physical fitness gains you've already made*. It's always an attention getter and a clear "running up the colors" on your personal masthead to say that you're quite purposely acting as attractively as you can.

This signaling changes everything. Everyone at work looks at you differently now. The consensus is that you're either going up the ladder, or finding a new ladder to go up. With your social group, dressing better than the rest of the group flags you as a highly attractive and desirable member of the opposite sex. You will start pulling interest from others in Phase Three and that will have a direct effect on your primary partners' interest in you.

It's one thing knowing you have a decent husband and it's another thing knowing that two or three other women think he'd make a nice upgrade on their own husband. Alternatively, perhaps he'd be a good option for something short and exciting.

It's one thing knowing your wife is cute. It's another thing seeing other guys look her over and noticing that the fifteen pounds she lost in the gym were all the bad ones and none of the good ones.

Generally your clothing should be the best quality garments you can afford, appropriate to your location. Don't wear a suit to the Laundromat unless you run it or own it. Wearing track pants to the gym is fine, but not to your in-laws for Sunday lunch.

A nice rule of thumb is to dress a little better than everyone else does in your peer group.

Hey, Me Too

If the Vampire can't beat you, they'll join you.

Instead of sabotaging you like they did in Phase Two, they will often suddenly start trying to increase their own value. The hope to pull you back down to Phase Two by evening the attractiveness score between the two of you.

That's why they are suddenly so interested in the gym. That's why they are suddenly doing an amazing job at work. That's why your social group is doing something impressive. They are trying to trump you and regain their #1 spot.

Also at this point, they will typically become far more engaging and interested in giving you what you want, while still trying to protect whatever it is that they really need from you. Sometimes they'll bend over backwards to give you anything you want... except that one thing you really want them to change.

Therefore, it's... *"I'll cook for you, I'll have sex, I'll find a part-time job, I'll visit your mother in the hospital, I'll let you choose where we go on vacation. Just don't make me stop being an alcoholic!"*

In terms of employers, the classic way of playing the "Me Too" game is by using a variant where they start claiming credit for your ideas and methods. You're doing amazing work and your boss represents it as their own influence.

Your social group adopts your ideas and concerns, but owns it as something only the group leadership can execute cleanly and they don't invite you in to take part in it. So if your thing was turning the school play into a video and you have a camera and equipment, it's accepted as a great idea, but magically someone else was hired to tape it and complete your idea.

The Test

There's always a test.

Repeat. There's ALWAYS a test.

If you've started getting yourself together physically and you've started being a little flirty and fun, someone out there is going to throw themself at you sexually.

If you're a reasonably attractive woman, you're used to men making passes at you, so will have little sense of shock when it happens. In fact, you'll quite enjoy them most likely.

It's the men and women who aren't used to being desirable that truly struggle with the test. Invariably it's someone that you've known for a long time and always been interested in (don't lie to me, I know the tune here) who unexpectedly throws sexual interest in your direction.

She hasn't been anything other than a friend or co-worker with no interest in you "that way" and suddenly she's giggly and twirling her hair at you, asking what you're doing this weekend.

It's the good-looking dad in a suit picking up his daughter from school, who strikes up a playful conversation. Then he asks if you'd like to get some coffee sometime.

If you've been suffering a long drought of genuine attention, affection or admiration, that's going to be very tempting to follow up on. It's very easy to find yourself drawn to other people who want you the way you want to be wanted.

If you're married, trust me on this, there's always some other woman that makes herself available to guys running the MAP before the wife fully responds. There's always a player on the prowl for lonely wives before the husband wakes up. Just expect it to happen and treat it like a positive sign you're getting things heading on the right path. Don't take the detour. The moral high ground is very important in later MAP Phases if you have to go that far.

In terms of social groups and employers, there are always other social groups and employers that can express an interest or advertise for open positions. If you're going to flip through the help wanted ads, or surf the Internet for a new job, don't bring the paper to work or register with your work email.

State Your Intentions .

In Phase Three, you can get increasingly verbally blunt about what you want from your relationship. You can start making firm verbal demands that the Vampire stop being a Vampire and start acting like a responsible relationship partner to you.

For most men running the MAP for primary relationship reasons, this is when your partner finally starts apologizing and acting right. Women tend to respond very positively to a man who is more attractive than they are, giving them clear relationship expectations and standards. They will verbally test that and become upset for a day or two, but very much tend to come around fairly quickly.

Unfortunately, for women running the MAP for primary relationship reasons, odds are that he won't get it from you just talking to him. I hate to say it, but it's very common that the husband doesn't listen very well to mere talk and will need the bucket of cold water of Phase Four thrown at him. It's a very common pattern for things to play out that way.

Certainly though, whoever is on the other end of the relationship, they should have a pretty clear idea what your primary relationship concerns are by halfway into Phase Three.

Timing the Move to Phase Four

All in all, Phase Three is going to last about three to six months.

Phase Three lasts until you purposely push it to Phase Four, though I suggest you let it run for at least two or three months before moving there. If you go too quickly into Phase Four, you may not have given your Vampire enough time to mentally process the difference and adjust to things.

Phase Three is actually rather enjoyable compared to Phase Two, so it's tempting to stall out here and not force the issue by going to Phase Four. However if you wait too long, you're sending the message that you really are very reluctant to force the issue and are emotionally dependent on the Vampire still. The Vampire will correctly interpret as you being weak to them and assume it's because they are always going to be better than you. You risk by inaction framing the Vampire as the true power in the relationship and sliding all the way back to Phase One.

If you think you are in Phase Three and the Vampire still is denying you what you need, you should push to Phase Four within about six months. Failure to push to a timely Phase Four can cost you a resetting of the entire process as you slide back to Phase One. However, if you repeatedly cycle between acting as if you might leave them and then backing down, you're training them to think you're always bluffing.

You can't bluff in the MAP. All in or all out.

"There's always a test.

Repeat. There's always a test."

Chapter 17 – Phase Four

Definition

Phase Four – If the verbal requests in Phase Three fail, you can move to Phase Four and give clear demonstrations of unhappiness with the relationship by your actions. You're displaying the willingness to end the relationship if the Vampire doesn't start to act right. This is a very short phase.

The Less You Say the Better

Having reached Phase Three, you're already in a position where you no longer directly need your Vampire. You've already talked at length about your case for them to make changes, and failed to get them to act. By moving to Phase Four, you're moving from talk to action.

You can and should continue to say what you want, but with the understanding that the more you talk, the weaker your case gets. Summarize your essential demand down to a single sentence... two at the most. The less you say in Phase Four the more powerful it is.

"If you can't stop drinking, it's over."

"I need a pay raise, or I have to find other work."

"If you can't be honest about the money, I can't stay."

"I want you to close the business and find a paying job, or I'm going to leave you."

"If you don't stop hanging out with the divorced party-girl troop until 3am, I need to find someone who wants to be with me."

The less you say, the stronger it is.

Often Phase Four is a Moment

Quite often Phase Four isn't exactly a planned event. Frequently the Vampire does something wildly inappropriate and you just mentally snap, and you find yourself delivering the "one sentence" line with incredible force and commitment.

You come home, he's drunk and the kid has been crying in the crib with a wet diaper for who knows how long and...

"If you can't stop drinking it's over."

BOOM! There it is. Phase Four. Cold. Hard. Real.

Here's the kicker though - often you aren't even mad about it when it clicks into Phase Four. It's as if someone throws a switch in your head as the realization hits you like a ton of bricks. *He's never going to stop drinking.* All there is for the future is what it's like now, with no hope for an actual change.

I know that might sound like an impossible feeling to have if you're someone in Phase One or Two, but that's because you still need them so much. When you're into Phase Three, you won't actually need them like you do now and when someone you don't need blows up crap in your life... you won't feel like you need to put up with it.

In fact, if you want, you can even say your one sentence as your own realization. Just let it hang in the air as a statement.

"You're never going to stop drinking, are you?"

The point is though, when you reach Phase Four, even if the moment takes you by surprise, you have to follow through on it.

"They always call your bluff. Therefore, you can't ever be bluffing."

Yes Dear for 48 Hours

What usually happens with a Phase Four demand, is that your Vampire apologizes and gives you immediate and quite pleasing compliance to your demands... *for 48 hours.*

They pour away all the alcohol.

They get some extra help in to cover the workload in your department.

The social group says that's a great idea and thanks, we'll put that into the meeting minutes to address next month.

You get laid twice and it's not just sex, it's really amazing wake the neighbors sex.

You think that this is all great, then after 48 hours, *everything reverts to exactly how it was before*. Leaving you standing there like Cinderella holding a pumpkin and four mice. They bought you off.

The Vampire will nearly always make this over-the-top effort to suck up to you to lull you back into passivity. Just watch for it and enjoy it as well as you can, but don't let your guard down. This "strong sucking up" is frequently referred to as "Hoovering".

The Phase Four Flop

If you reach Phase Four and then fail to follow through, you're flopping and that's a very damaging thing.

They will always call your bluff to see if you're really going to stick with your resolve. They comply for 48 hours to calm you down and then they test your resolve again to see if you are truly serious about what you want. If you fail to hold firm on what you said, they will perceive you as being weak to them and that you'll stick around and keep doing what they want you to do. Which means, if you pull a Phase Four moment and then back down from what you said, you're really all the way back in Phase One again.

If they cry because you said a "mean and nasty" Phase Four statement, don't comfort them. Just let them cry. They are in the wrong. You are in the right. If a bully wants your lunch money and you say no and the bully cries, you wouldn't comfort them.

If they call you a bad person, just brush it off. *"It's unfortunate that you feel that way, but [Phase Four statement]"*.

If they threaten you or suggest they will self-harm, offer to call 911.

The Fake Phase Four

This is where you make your Phase Four-like demand in a very weak, almost questioning manner. It's as if you're testing them to see how a real Phase Four would play out. You're throwing out a feeler and as soon as they smack it down, you can deny you were really testing them out.

This sort of thing is usually done in Phase Three and unless you are getting an immediate positive response to it the very first time you try it, odds are good that you're weakening your overall position. They will usually just automatically call your bluff and smack the Fake Phase Four down. If you give them practice smacking your Fake Phase Four's down, that gives them greater confidence to smack down the actual Phase Four when you finally get around to doing it.

Instead of being the boy that cried wolf, you're the wife that cried get a job.

No More Nice

Phase Four is the hinge of the MAP where you stop acting nice and start being willing to break the rules of being polite and cooperative.

The odds are that you're a nice person, so acting in a very impolite manner is probably not going to come easily to you, but you have to try because *nice hasn't worked* up until now.

The ugly truth is that some people, and I rather have to groan a little here and say that by "some people", I mean "husbands", simply don't get how bad things are, until the bad things are really happening. In four years of coaching and thousands of people helped, I've yet to have a husband ask for help because his wife said she was unhappy, but I do have a huge wave of panicked men saying they were worried their wife was cheating or had filed for divorce... *"Out of the blue."*

The solution is that you have to back up your Phase Four statement with action serious enough to gain real attention, while still not causing critical relationship damage. Some suggestions...

Separate the bedrooms.

Remove your wedding rings.

Ask them to move out.

Tell them you are not in love with them anymore.

Lock them out of your online presence and communication devices.

If you're a woman, have either his father or your father tell him you're on the verge of leaving him. Yes, it's sexist, but the combination of an authority figure + not a "white noise" female talking, often breaks through to men. I'm just saying what works in reality here.

Tell them you are starting to consider sex with other people.

Investigate your state's divorce / alimony / child support laws, and figure out the math on what they would likely have to live on based on a 50/50 custody agreement and non-combative parting of the ways.

It's a little harder to make dramatic moves with an employer or social group, but simply refusing to assist with non-mandated activities can often be effective.

If you have a case, head to Human Resources or go over your supervisor's head to report inappropriate or unfair conditions of your employment.

Make calls to the appropriate authorities to report legitimate concerns.

Whatever it is you do to act out, ensure that it's legal, non-violent, but as assertive as possible. You're actively trying to make trouble to make your point. You aren't trying to be nasty or vengeful, just demonstrating the line drawn in the sand. You've been seeking a peaceful resolution all along, but they have forced you into escalating things to this level. It's reasonable to act unreasonable about unreasonable treatment. You don't just smile and nod when someone you don't need treats you poorly.

I would also recommend doing several of those options in one heavy hitting strike. Your goal is to hit them so hard, it makes them sit up and take it seriously, yet you are making sure that it's a non-fatal blow. You don't want additional problems to clean up, just to freak them out enough to get into action and start changing things.

Writing letters may occasionally help in a primary relationship, but never use that method for an employer. It always goes up the chain of command and pisses off someone high up. Then they fire you.

What Happens After That

It's really a case of watching them carefully to see how they react after the first 48 hours has passed. If you see a compliant 48 hours and then everything starting to revert to normal, then you know Phase Four has failed to break through to them and you head into Phase Five.

You absolutely should know within a week at the very most whether they are going to wake up and take things seriously. If a week out they are continuing to turn things around and start putting it right, you've probably had a successful Phase Four.

As always though, you can't make people do anything, only influence their behavior. If you push to Phase Four, you absolutely have to follow through on it. It's a very stressful time in any relationship but there's no going backwards at this point. You have to go forward.

Chapter 18 – Phase Five

Definition

Phase Five – If Phase Four fails, you begin to withdraw your support from the Vampire and let natural consequences of that lack of support manifest. You begin getting your ducks in a row for a potential exit from the relationship.

Give Up On Them Changing

This is a very hard Phase for you emotionally, because your Vampire, who you love or at the very least have history with, has now proved they aren't interested in you beyond what they can get from you. That hurts.

When you give up on them changing, you have to let go of all of your emotions about them. Not only the negative emotions like anger, guilt and hate, but also the positive ones like affection and love. The more emotional you are about them, the more leverage they will have over you. The opposite of love isn't hate, it's indifference, so become indifferent to them.

The less emotionally connected to them you are, the less needy you appear. Your need for them has helped create the entire scenario where you're their Victim. By giving up on the idea that they will change, you're also giving up hope that they will treat you well at some point in the future.

If they have any need for you, when you start shutting off and withdrawing from them, that's going to make them alarmed that you might actually leave in reality. Very likely, they will start to pursue you. It sounds like a dark tactic, but they have driven you to this point after being nice about it got you nothing.

Plan Your Exit

During Phase Five you start getting all your ducks in a row for your ultimate exit from the relationship if needed.

If this is a primary partner relationship, do things like opening a personal bank account and seek legal advice for how things will play out. Make copies of any important records and keep them in a safe place. Remove any items of special personal interest that you worry may be ruined or lost should things turn dramatic. Now is also not the time to have firearms in the house. A spare set of car keys may be amazingly helpful should someone hurl them somewhere in a fit of rage. At this point, you're trying to salvage what you can from the wreckage of being with someone who doesn't love you.

If this is some other kind of social group relationship or employment, keep all the records up to date, absolutely ensure that you are playing by the rules, to the letter of the law, not giving them an opportunity to punish you on a technicality. If they think you're leaving no matter what, it's common to face disciplinary action for minor things you would never have received discipline for earlier. It's a change of policy just for you.

Because you've given up, you're no longer trying to actively court them to change their behavior. Your goal now is simply to plan a low-key, peaceful exit from whatever relationship you have.

Give Them a Taste of You Being Gone

By this point, the Vampire has realized that they need you. Failing to supply them with what they need you for can be very educational.

The natural consequences of them driving you away, is that you'll be gone. If you keep saving them from something they should be handling, stop rescuing them. If they can't drive themselves to work because they can't drive, don't drive them. Tell them they need to learn to drive. When they get mad about it, do nothing.

161

If you're the one bankrolling everything, figure out what the after-the-relationship finances would be and only give them that to live on.

Stop socializing with them for fun and start socializing with others.

Don't scurry about getting their dry cleaning, making them special lunches and doing all the chores.

In a sense, you're going on a relationship strike as you stop caring about them and start worrying about you and your exit. You obviously shouldn't move this into unethical or unsafe behavior, but certainly bring things down to the very minimum of relationship comfort building behavior.

You stay friendly, but also firm and polite. *"No I'm not going to do that. You need to figure that out for yourself."*

Phase Five as an employee is tricky, trying to balance the task refusals and yet not get yourself in trouble for something unrelated to the real issue of your employment. If you have to face discipline as an over-the-top response about something unrelated, that's a good sign that you have to go to Phase Six. If so, try to fall off the "must be disciplined" radar of people above you.

If you're an employee, when something is clearly in another person's job description, refuse to do it for him or her. Cover your ass with something written prompting them to complete the task. Be polite but firm about it. Only when something is clearly inappropriate do you want to make a fuss about it.

"Sometimes it's only as you give up on them, that they realize they want you."

But Think of the Children!

If this is a primary relationship where kids are involved and you start giving them a taste of what it's going to be like without you around, watch for the Vampire making the needs of the children suddenly become far more comprehensive than before.

Obviously you're still going to take care of your kids, but because your need isn't working to control you anymore, the needs of the children become the new leverage. Suddenly everything they want routes through what you have to do for the children, by framing you as a bad parent by default. The irony is that the better parent you are, the more emotional leverage calling you a bad parent has over you.

In terms of handling it, absolutely ensure that the health and safety of the children are a priority, but do pay close attention to things "for the children" that are suddenly springing up as new tasks or expenses for you. It's not a requirement that children are entertained and pampered to excess 24/7. There's no requirement to turn your house into Disney World.

The other way they use children as human shields, is by blaming you for all the bad side effects of divorce that will affect them. This is an important concern and typically an argument that carries a lot of weight, because you've probably already considered that yourself. In fact, the children are very often the exact reason the Victim delays dealing with their Vampire for several years longer than necessary. Often your greatest fear is leaving the children unsupervised with the Vampire.

What it comes down to is exactly how bad the bad stuff is. By the time you're in Phase Five, you're not here because you have a trivial concern like, *"I'm only getting sex four times a week and I'd like it to be five times a week."* Whatever the concern is that's driven you to this point, it's something that's clearly inappropriate and actively bad for you to be around. You can't just let yourself be a victim of cheating, or hit, verbally abused, driven into bankruptcy by their spending and just take it on the chin endlessly. It's utterly toxic.

There is no one-size-fits-all set of advice here as to whether or not you should be pushing the MAP this far. I'm simply describing the process to maximize your chances of success if you go this way.

The Power of the Takeaway

Because they actually need you and you aren't bluffing that you're willing to walk, it's potentially a wake-up moment for the Vampire.

The irony is that by the time you're in Phase Five, there's a role reversal happening. You have what they need and you don't need what they have. That casts you in the role of the Vampire and them in the role of the Victim... all the way back in their Phase One.

The purpose of Phase Five is to provide them with a sufficient dose of reality, to show them they aren't in the driver's seat anymore. You're the one in charge making the rules and demands. You're also heading to a place where if they don't comply, they are the one who will be ejected from the relationship. If they need you like they are in a Phase One, they have a lot of internal pressure to bow to your demand to correct the relationship breaking issue.

It's okay to be a little bit mean about it too. Remember you tried nice all the way through Phases One, Two and Three. Nice didn't work. Being blunt might work. Not nasty and vicious, just not nice.

Slow Motion

Phase Five sounds rather callous and calculating, but it is a vastly superior way of approaching a final ultimatum (Phase Six) than the usual method of getting there. Most relationships end in an explosion of sorts where Phase Four and Phase Six blur together in an emotional eruption, with no Phase Five at all. The relationship reaches the critical tipping point where someone flips out and they nuke the entire relationship into the ground less than a second later.

Compare these two approaches...

"You're never going to look for work are you? I want a divorce NOW!" and then handing them divorce papers within 48 hours.

"You're never going to look for work are you?" One-week review of behavior, removing of wedding rings, separating the beds, etc. Then a multi-month Phase Five where the finances somewhat are separated and there is no further catering to the other spouse. Then you are heading to Phase Six and divorce.

The truth is most people don't rationally intend to get divorced. They have no plan to approach it and use it as a threat to change behavior in their spouse, *they just flip out one day and blow it up.* By slowing the rush to ending the relationship down, it gives time for the other person to come to their senses and agree to make changes.

Checking Out

The one great risk to Phase Five is that you really do check out of the relationship and stop caring.

In general, the further through the phases of the MAP you go, the more checked out you tend to be. It's really nice if they respond in Phase Two, because that means you feel like they really love you and they were just waiting for you to pull your act together. Phase Three isn't so warm and fuzzy, but it's still fine. Once you're into Phase Four, Five or Six before they respond, it really starts becoming a little bit hurtful that you had to turn into an ogre. You would hope they would care about you enough to hold up their end of the relationship without you needing to go through all this.

Once your feelings for them die, they don't always come back quickly and easily. If you're still hooked into your Vampire in an earlier Phase, it probably sounds impossible to stop caring intensely about them. The reality is though, that once you are into your MAP this deeply, you may find it hard to care about them at all.

It's worth verbalizing that to them at some point. The *I love you, but I'm not in love with you* speech is a classic.

If You're Just Done

If you already know that you're just done with the whole situation no matter what they do, you still may not be in the immediate situation where you can leave. Maybe you need some cash to make a break for it, or need another job lined up, or to find a new social group to be involved with.

If you just plan to exit the plane and pop a chute, stay quiet and be as cooperative and low-key as possible. Then head to Phase Six when you can.

Chapter 19 – Phase Six

Definition

Phase Six – An Option A or B ultimatum is given to the Vampire. Option A means the Vampire complies with your demands. Option B means the relationship is ended.

Option A or B

Phase Six drives the relationship to its final resolution by forcing a clearly defined choice on the Vampire, to either behave appropriately, or face the end of the relationship.

Option A is the choice where they decide to conform to the demands of the ultimatum. These demands need to be explicitly stated and clearly understood. Some examples of Option A demands are things like...

Going completely no contact with an affair partner.
Allowing open access to communication devices.
Getting medical treatment for illness or addiction.
Improved working conditions.
Improved pay.
Apology for wrongdoing.
Begin a fitness regime and stick to it.
Ending some form of offensive behavior in the group.
Begin counseling.

These always have a direct relation to the relationship breaking issues raised in Phase Four.

Option B is the choice where they decide not to conform to the demands of the ultimatum and the relationship ends. So that means things like filing for divorce, putting in your notice at work, or resigning from whatever the social group is requiring of you.

Have the Paperwork Ready

When you do Phase Six, always have the paperwork ready for both Option A and B.

If there is the possibility that you would divorce, you need to have that divorce paperwork ready for signing by your partner during the Phase Six discussion. This is both so it clarifies in your own mind what you are committing yourself to and because it's vastly stronger if you're displaying clear commitment to following through on your ultimatum.

If there is the possibility of putting in your notice at work or needing to resign from something, have that letter prewritten before your meeting. Again, it's clarifying for you to do it and can end a great deal of awkward debate nearly instantly the moment you hand it over.

It's also important to have any and all of the Option A paperwork ready too. If your demand was to start marriage counseling, or have your partner see a doctor for their medical issue, have the numbers on hand to book the appointments during the meeting, or already have them booked. Likewise, if there are clear tasks and goals you want met to stay in the relationship, have those written out in advance.

Ideally, you should have two packets of paperwork or materials ready for the meeting, one for Option A and one for Option B. There should be no confusion about the choice you're putting to them.

Plan for Personal Space

Any final ultimatum on a long relationship is going to be emotionally taxing. Even if they take Option A the experience is going to be emotionally Draining.

Plan ahead as best you can to time the meeting for when there's going to be as much of a lull as you can get in your week. If you do it in the middle of a high pressure moment, you run the risk of the ultimatum failing more easily or simply having everything come to a more dramatic end.

Also, allow for taking physical space away from each other. There's often going to be a level of disbelief and shock when the ultimatum is finally given. Giving them 48 hours to consider things is fine, but it's also well worth planning that you have personal space available to both parties during that time.

Incidentally, this 48-hour cool down is why Human Resources departments prefer to fire people on a Friday. It gives the fired employee the whole weekend to calm down and mentally regroup.

Affair Busting Caveat

The caveat to personal space during Option A or B is if you're seeking to end an affair that your primary partner is having. In that case, your demands are typically to break off all contact with their affair partner, expose the affair to the other spouse and full access to your partner's communication devices. If you back away and give them space, they typically immediately seek out their affair partner and make plans to drive it underground.

Affair busting is somewhat beyond the scope of this book, but ending affairs always requires a very firm and direct intervention with heavy duty follow up.

Say Goodbye and Thank You

Especially in primary relationships, if you're about to break up, another tactic that may work as a last ditch effort, is to contact your partner's family and closest friends and tell them what is going on and request their assistance in trying to influence them toward choosing Option A.

It's probably best to do this as a short letter, or email, where you explain what has happened up to this point and explain that they have a choice

169

to make. Say that you want to save the relationship, but also say that you aren't willing to tolerate what is currently happening either. Most people will still be sympathetic to your case if you've been asking for nothing more than what is reasonable from your partner.

For your in-laws, you should also thank them for anything that they have done for you over the years and express sadness that if your relationship ends, the relationship with them will change as well. Thanking is extremely important because it shows you're not being emotionally hostile, and it goes a long way to disarming your in-laws from feeling angry with you. Relationships typically end either "sad or mad", so you thanking them frames it as being sad.

When you expose the real reason for ending things and your willingness to make it work with reasonable demands, it hampers their ability to spin you as the bad guy in the relationship. You were the good partner that got screwed over, yet you honorably and gracefully withdrew from the relationship.

If you're displaying higher value than your partner, very often your in-laws will attempt to reason with your partner behind the scenes and argue your case.

In workplace or social groups, the people you say goodbye to are your mentors, people who hired you and friends in your group. It's the same thing as in-laws in that you're trying to leave sad rather than mad. There's no point burning bridges will individual people on the way out, these are people you can go to for references in the future and so on.

If you're a person of quality, your mentors can also be extremely concerned about your leaving and can potentially pull strings behind the scenes to assist your situation. Maybe that's dealing with your current problem, maybe that's helping you exit more smoothly to a new opportunity. Either way, they can be very helpful.

"Relationships end either sad or mad."

Keep the Moral High Ground

It's always extremely important to keep the moral high ground. By the time Phase Six is happening, you're exhausted of dealing with the relationship and likely getting other opportunities thrown your way.

It's always going to be tempting to take some kind of revenge action against them, if only from frustration. Whether that's cheating on them, ruining some social event they were at, slandering them on Facebook, failing to complete job assignments properly, stealing or whatever else you can think of... don't do it.

All vengeful action does is damage any ability to fix things properly should they come around to Option B, or damage your ability to have a happy Option A.

This is The Last Resort

Just so we're clear on this, pushing to Phase Six is the very last resort for trying to resolve things. You've exhausted all the other options for trying to gain their attention and willingness to work with you. They don't want a proper relationship with you. You're not the bad guy.

If you're trapped in an ultimatum cycle of seeing results and then it all reverting back to how it was before, you need to stop it. Second, third and fourth ultimatums just get progressively less effective and less meaningful. You're going to be better off just ending things and moving on as opposed to endlessly threatening to leave.

If you're just done with them, then you're done. By the time you hit Phase Six you may not even want Option A to be available to them. If so, just go the Option B route as gracefully as you can. This is far more likely with an employment situation than a primary relationship, but if you offer an Option A, you have to expect they may take it. If you then turn it down, it just causes drama and angry feelings with no net gain for you.

But My Religion Forbids Divorce

This is a hard situation for many people. You're in a truly horrible marriage that is clearly not in your best personal interest to be in, but also struggling with the religious requirement to never divorce. That's a terrible double bind in that you lose whether you stay in the marriage or not.

The real twist is that often your Vampire is completely aware of how your religious beliefs trap you. In fact, your religious commitment can be the very thing that has allowed your Vampire to feel empowered enough to control you. They will also use scriptures and your religious leadership to provide pressure on you to stay as a loyal, obedient spouse.

I don't want to try to talk you out of your faith, but I will say that I've seen a large number of people faced with that dilemma, decide to push to an ultimatum and have a very positive result from it. When you decide to break the double bind, it releases a great deal of energy back into your life and changes your relationship greatly. More often than not, the Vampire spouse is happier for it too.

I've had clients who refused to push for an ultimatum and then had their spouse file for divorce on them anyway. The core issue in those cases is the endless displaying of low value making the divorcing spouse lose interest. I've also seen failure to take strong action turn into the other spouse having an affair. No one likes living with a spineless spouse.

I really do understand how it's a questionable area for some people. All I'm trying to say is that I respect that and sympathize, but I've also seen a Phase Six made about obviously serious issues, work really well. If everything else has failed, the MAP is worth using as a final option.

"Making a divorce threat without the paperwork ready for signing, is just a lot of yelling."

Chapter 20 – Phase Seven

Definition

Phase Seven – You transition to a life without a Vampire.

How You Get Here

You can arrive at Phase Seven directly from any of the other Phases. Essentially, at the point your Vampire decides to stop being your Vampire and is willing to be an equal partner, you arrive at Phase Seven.

The other way you get here is when the Vampire decides in Phase Six that they will never give you what you need from your relationship with them.

No matter how you get to Phase Seven, it always represents a major shift in your overall energy levels.

Reaching Phase Seven means that one of your life's most pressing problems has been resolved and that is a huge piece of the puzzle of moving up to a higher energy set. Often you've spent a lot of effort in raising the rest of your life to that higher energy set and the resolution of your major problem is the capstone to all that effort.

Winning the War

It's important to recognize when Phase Seven arrives, because you can misstep and immediately bounce back to an earlier phase, if you don't notice you won the war.

What happens is that at some point your Vampire admits defeat and agrees to your terms, which means you won the war. However if you keep fighting the war, they think they have a chance to win it back. Moreover, they feel the need to defend themselves, so the war resumes.

Any time you negotiate to get something you want from someone, if they agree to grant your wish, STOP FIGHTING THEM. You've already closed the deal. Stop yapping. Just let it sit.

Seriously. Just zip your lip. You got them to agree to what you wanted, so stop trying to convince them further that you should get what you want. You already have the *yes* you want, so all that can happen if you keep talking to them, is that you give them a reason to change their mind to a *no*.

It doesn't matter whether you're a kid asking to go to a party, an employee asking for a promotion, or a wife asking her husband to go to the doctor. You're asking for something, they said *yes*. Don't hear the *yes* and then explain that saying *yes* is a great deal because...

...Mike's brother was the one that bought all the beer to the party last year and he's not coming because he's in jail now. So it's cool right?

...that you're the only one in the whole agency that can operate the old TPS Machine and the new ones aren't being delivered for nine months. So you're valuable right?

...that you've been talking to all your girlfriends about Mr. Droopy and they all agree that you really have to see a doctor. So you're going right?

Right?

No, you can't go to the party. What happened last year? What did Mike's brother do to go to jail? Who is Mike anyway?!

No at this point, you're just too valuable working the old TPS machine. There's just no way we could move you until the new ones arrive.

What do you mean you talked to everyone about that?! WHY WOULD YOU SAY THAT TO EVERYONE? I DON'T HAVE A PROBLEM, IT'S ONLY BEEN HAPPENING FOR A YEAR!

See why if you get your *yes,* you just stop talking?

You won the war!

It's Finally Over

If your relationship ends via an Option B Phase Six, it's going to be sad, but at least it's finally over.

You'll sleep easy knowing you gave it your all and gave them every chance to turn it around. You took the high road on the way out. You didn't lie, cheat or do anything other than give them the best you possibly could, and it wasn't enough for them.

The good news is that by the time you've arrived finally at Phase Seven, you'll be in the best place possible to find someone or something new to fill your life with happiness and success. You're in great shape, economically sound, displaying high value, able to love, know and care for yourself and able to have a positive sexual relationship. You're battle-tested and as hot as you'll ever be. You will have other opportunities.

However, you can also experience a huge emotional letdown after the adrenaline begins to fade and fall into a depression. You've pushed for so long, for so hard and now, it's finally over and there's nothing left for you to give. What's been holding you up for the longest time was your Vampire resisting you and with the resistance gone, you collapse.

The good news is this bottoming out is temporary. As you recover your strength, you'll start to feel much better than you have for a long time. Just go easy on yourself for a couple of months. It will be fine.

"Phase Seven is just the beginning of a higher-level energy set. It can get even better after this!"

175

Winning the Peace

Whether you won the war, or it's just finally over, you now have to win the peace.

Whatever the situation was with your relationship, you have to do something very difficult. You have to let the past go. You can't hold it over them forever. You have to forgive the past and move into the future. You can keep the score even between you from here forward, but you can't even the score for what happened in the past.

Up until this point, your negative emotions about the situation were likely motivating factors in propelling you forward. You were mad, so you worked out like crazy in the gym, for example. You were if nothing else, focused on moving yourself forward and winning the war. The emotions were negative, but the goal was very positive, getting you a net positive. Having won the war though, all of those negative emotions will turn toxic without the outlet of the positive goal. All you have left is mentally reviewing the failures of the past.

The goal was to be in a proper relationship, so having arrived on the cusp of having one, you need to allow it to transition to a proper relationship.

The Rage Volcano

It's extremely common for the Victim to finally gain compliance from their Vampire, only to have the Victim explode in a volcano of rage that frankly surprises even themselves. This can undo a great deal of positive progress in less than a minute.

What happens is that when the ex-Vampire starts doing what they should have been doing all along, the ex-Victim often feels a wave of disgust at having let the Vampire take advantage of them for so long. The longer the relationship was taking advantage of them, the greater the rage. If all it took to undo years of a husband ignoring his wife's sexual advances was a trip to the doctor and a testosterone shot, to see him suddenly happy and horny, *like nothing was ever wrong*, turns the wife livid. All those years he denied her and he could have gone to the doctor the whole time... BOOM! Rage Volcano.

It's normal.

It's going to hit.

You just have to expect it to hit at random and call it for what it is when it hits. It's not that you hate them. It's that you love them and want to be loved by them too.

The trick is to step back from yourself and just allow the wave of emotion to pass through you. It's often a huge ball of negative energy locked inside you behind a firewall of pain and sorrow. It may even hit more than once.

Verbalize the emotions you're experiencing *to* your primary partner, but not *at* them. Be honest about what you are experiencing, but make it about the situation, rather than about your partner. Remember you've played your own role in creating the things that happened. It's as much about self-hatred as it is about hating them. Just have a big old victim puke and you'll feel better.

On the other side of the rage volcano is peace.

The Old is Dead, Live the New

Whatever your old relationships were, they are over. Whatever your relationships are now are new ones.

With couples in particular, when both sides of the relationship decide to run the MAP together, both stop their Reds, fix their Yellows and live their Greens... the changes can be awe inspiring. Not only do individuals have their own energy sets, couples in sexual relationships make up major pieces of the puzzle in each other's energy set. Your partner becoming more attractive and high-energy makes you become more attractive and high-energy more easily. This is also why you don't want to punish them into the future and bring them down with negative emotion. If you can feel positive about them, they can more easily lift you up too.

You also have to consider how much of your identity was invested in being their Victim and how much of theirs was tied up in being the Vampire. You can second-guess them being a nice partner even when they are being nice to you. You can feel lost and wonder what it is that you do now that you're not a Victim and Vampire.

It's a process of learning your new life. As you flip from one energy set to a higher one, you're going to have to learn new ways of being yourself. If your life together keeps getting better and better, you may go through multiple events of self-improvement and energy set switching. All of this will require you to be open to learning new ways to be your best self.

Out of the Frying Pan

Something to be careful about in the early days of Phase Seven is making big decisions or getting involved in new serious relationships.

There's always the desire to be in relationships, but you tend to attract people to you at your current energy level. If you're just exhausted from fighting your way to Phase Seven, your energy is going to be low simply from tiredness. Be cautious about attracting someone new to you with a low-energy level.

It will feel great at the time, but as you continue to feel more yourself, your new relationship may be as fraught with issues as your old one was. If you give yourself a few months to get your head together, it may save you a lot of grief over the long term.

New Energy and Upward Momentum

All the dangers in Phase Seven come summarize to one thing, accidentally finding a new way to self-sabotage and drive yourself back down to a lower energy set. The first year after reaching Phase Seven is critical in that you want to create a positive upward momentum.

Relationship momentum is a critical thing to understand. It doesn't matter where you are right now in your relationships; *it matters where you are going*. You're better off being in a bad relationship that is getting better, than a good relationship that is getting worse. Once relationships are heading in a direction, they tend to keep heading in that direction.

As tempting as it may seem to take a break and just enjoy having reached Phase Seven, that's the attitude of resting in place that very likely caused your problems in the first place. What you really must do is not give up making progress. The hardest part of the battle is completed, you've halted the downward momentum but now you must create an upward momentum.

All it may take is a year or two of truly hard effort and it can result in decades of happiness and stability. Once things are heading upwards, there's no reason they can't just keep getting slowly better and better, without having to do much more than show up and put in some regular positive effort. It's always harder to get something started than to keep it going once its running. Things can take on a life of their own after a while and get stronger all by themselves.

Save you. Save them. Save everyone.

You can do this.

Chapter 21 – The Rest of Your Life

The MAP is a Lifestyle

The MAP never really ends. To be sure, you can push hard for a year or two to turn things around, but overall you're still going to keep doing the MAP for the rest of your life.

Your physical health will only become more and more concerning as you get older. It's nice to be twenty-years-old and physically fit, but to be in good shape at sixty-years-old is a huge positive. At some point, you run out of the ability to do meaningful work, so your retirement income is even more important than your working income. Everything in the MAP are things you should have been doing anyway. The MAP is just a way of organizing everything into coherent and positive plan for your future.

There is no end to the MAP, but it's not always going to be "more of the same". As you improve yourself more and more, you will find there are plateaus and new peaks to hit in every area of your life. With the right partner, sex can be better at fifty than at twenty-five. You can travel more places, see new things, taste new food, listen to new music. You're not going to be bored, unless you're boring.

It's a very big world out there. You're not going to get to see it all before you die.

Don't Over Think Things

The MAP is always going to be one of those "easy to say, hard to do" things. So if you find yourself endlessly talking about the MAP, or trying to think about the MAP and what the right thing is or is not to do, you're not actually doing the MAP.

Everything comes down to your feelings.

If something makes you feel good when you do it, it's positive. If something makes you feel bad, it's negative. Concentrate on doing things that make you feel positive, stop the ones that make you feel negative.

Your energy will always be in some combination of Draining, Stagnant or Flowing. You stop, fix and do for each of the three energy states. You've always doing some sort of action, rather than sitting in a circle talking about it.

Choose Your Friends Wisely

Take your five closest friends and family members and average them into an imaginary composite person. That composite person is probably very close to your income, physical fitness, happiness, social status, sex life and nearly anything else you care to compare yourself.

Imagine you're a normal guy moving into a new town. If you make friends with four overweight computer gamers, you're probably going to start playing computer games and gaining weight. Yet, if you moved in and started hanging out with four gym rats who like mountain biking, you're probably going to start going to the gym and mountain biking.

The same sort of thing happens with the way people earn and spend money and it's a factor in how you think politically and religiously. It's very much a factor in the success of your primary relationship too. If your (or your partner's) four best friends all start divorcing, that creates a major destabilizing influence in your relationship whether you want it to or not.

It may sound rather cold, but the truth is that your inner circle deeply influences you on a multitude of levels you may barely be conscious of. You're part of a shared energy set. So choose wisely.

I'm not saying immediately shuck everyone from your life, but odds are good that you have one person in your life that you should probably drop contact with. When the least happy person goes, the average happiness of the group rises.

181

You don't have to drop everyone you know and look for a better inner circle to be part of, because there will be people around you that also have some upward momentum in their lives. Your success can beget their success and vice versa. There's not much better than having old friends who started with nothing, who now have something.

It's Okay to Have Things Go Right

Look carefully at yourself when things are going wrong. Ask yourself the very simple and clear question...

"Is there anything I could be doing to stop it from blowing up?"

It is quite common for people to complete 95% of a major task in their life and then just fail to complete the final hurdle. It's having a university degree completed, except for one final course. It's having a painting completed, just not yet framed. It's booking a plane flight for a dream vacation, then somehow getting to the airport too late and missing the flight.

If you have something you know you need to complete, don't even bother trying to figure out why you can't complete it. Just go complete it. Don't bother delving into a negative energy mindset further to figure it out, just complete the task and you'll feel better.

Half the time you're just frightened of success because it's an unknown to you. Some things in life you'll never be ready for until you've gotten yourself in waist deep and figure it out on the fly.

It's okay to have things go right.

"The universe responds to your actions."

Complaining Makes It Worse

Complaining about your circumstances never fixes anything, only action can fix things. Stop complaining and start doing something about it. Complaining is just an echo chamber of negative energy and what you send out just comes right back to you.

You usually feel worse after complaining, than you would if you had simply shrugged your shoulders and done nothing.

Often the first real sign that someone is going to make significant positive changes in their life is that they stop talking about how bad things are. The move from talking about change to changing is often a move to the silent execution of a plan. Say nothing about your change until someone asks you about the results they see in you.

Also, when you talk about needing change there's always going to be a group of people who tell you it's impossible and that you should just give up before you take a single step. It's easy to say that you should just ignore them, but the reality is that all the negative talk directed at you can take its toll on your motivation. However, if you don't tell them what you plan to do, you don't have to listen to them try to talk you out of it. By the time they realize you have positive results, they can only complain about your success, which is a lot easier to tolerate.

In terms of primary relationships, there's also a difference between talking about a problem in your day in search of a solution and merely complaining about it. It's a stereotype, but men tend to talk only when they want a solution and are confused when women only sympathize with them. While women tend to talk looking for sympathy rather than assistance with a solution and are annoyed when men offer one. It helps to clarify what your partner defines as "listening" before they start talking.

"Everything comes down to your feelings."

Look for the Silver Lining

As bad as things can get, there is always some kind of lesson or skill to gain from the experience.

Life isn't always easy and sometimes it's just grindingly hard. However even the worst experiences of your life, can be the most important ones for your long-term development. You can learn more from a failure or a defeat than you can from a victory. There is truth to the saying "no pain, no gain".

That is not to suggest you go looking for drama and bad situations, but once you are in choppy waters, figure out why you got there, what happened and how to get out. It also doesn't mean you stay in a bad situation to "learn more". There's no virtue in exposing yourself needlessly to pointless struggle. If you're in a bad place, get out of it.

Often it's only once you are well past the hard parts that you can look back over your life and see how the lessons you learned then are of value to you now. Finding the silver lining is good though, because it can give you a sense of peace and closure to a bad experience. It's a different thing to look back at failure and see not failure, but the foundations of today's success.

Once you have that mindset, it's easier to try things that could fail. Not everything will work, some things will fail, so it's tempting sometimes to not try because you might fail. It's tempting to play it safe, but if you can see in every failure a silver lining of wisdom, skill or knowledge, then failure becomes the foundation of success.

This makes you feel like you can't truly fail, it makes you feel confident, it makes you feel hopeful and energetic and makes you feel you can succeed and feelings are infectious, so when you believe in you, everyone else starts believing in you to.

Don't give up.

We Are Connected

The world is a magical place.

Once you start experimenting with making your life better, you'll start seeing the results of positive improvements in your life and primary relationship. You'll see results in wider groups like your friends and family too. Energy sets come in all sizes and cover your entire company, town, state, nation and ultimately the world.

We all have a connection as one mass of humanity. Even if those bonds are incredibly tiny, they are still there, pulling on one another ever so faintly in a giant fabric of intention and feeling.

Unquestionably, the vast majority of people you will meet in your life are simply random strangers, just as the vast majority of people who find my website are simply searching on Google. However, there are also going to be a handful of special moments where that connection we all share introduces you to someone you needed to meet. When you meet those people, you'll find those very fruitful learning experiences to latch onto.

You still have to put yourself out there and meet people, it's not like the people you need to meet come door to door, but there's nothing particularly special you have to do to meet them, other than be in action. Just be mindful when you meet people. It's always wonderful to meet someone who has a prepackaged silver lining for you, without you having to go through the drama of having to live it to learn it.

Have Some Faith

I believe the universe responds to your actions.

The MAP grounds itself in the practical, so at first glance it may not seem very spiritual. The MAP works for everyone regardless of religious belief or lack thereof, but as you move to a higher state of personal energy, it does start to feel subtly spiritual.

Being mindful of your actions is a common theme in most religious traditions. Being mindful of your mindset is common as well.

At times, the MAP can sound terribly selfish, but when you are your best self, you perform your best and do the most good you can do for the world. Having high-energy matters not just for you, but everyone else too.

The universe, or at the very least our planet, is a giant energy set. You may be simply one tiny speck in a sea of humanity, but your best actions can reverberate out into the lives of others. What you send out comes back eventually. While I don't believe in prayers magically supplying you with things you need, I do have a low-key faith in the universe being one giant reflective field of intention.

What you send out, can come back. It just takes time.

I've always believed that if I put out enough positive energy, helped enough people, was utterly truthful and genuine, that it would somehow return to my family and me. As the last few years have unfolded, I've experienced Flow States more frequently and had many remarkable connections with people and places. I could never have predicted how many lives I would have touched with my writing. For the last three years, I've had at least daily messages, thanking me for the MAP has changing their lives for the better.

One of the reasons I wrote this book, was because unexpected positive side effects kept happening when people ran the MAP. Call it a loose sort of faith, but I've just started to expect those unexpected positive effects.

Get into action, be your best self, be mindful, have some faith.

"Complaining about your circumstances never fixes anything, only action can fix things."

About the Author

Athol Kay was born in Wellington, New Zealand and has a degree in Sociology from Victoria University. In 1991 at the age of 21, he met his wife Jennifer while being the guest speaker at a religious retreat held at her college, Susquehanna University in Pennsylvania. After a three-year long distance courtship, they married in 1994 and have two teenage daughters.

A keen observer of the religious world, Athol intended to go into the ministry as a career, but after a crisis of faith, he left the church and abandoned ministry aspirations. Athol joined Jennifer in her work with the developmentally disabled, retrained as a nurse and spent from 1995 to 2012 working with developmentally disabled adults and behaviorally challenged teens.

A deeply intellectual person, Athol never stopped actively learning and independently read across multiple fields of research leading toward the creation of the *Married Man Sex Life* project in 2010. MMSL is a hybrid of evolutionary psychology, biological, sociology, sexuality and the first application of "dating coach" advice to married life. At first a blog and then a book, MMSL quickly gained a reputation for deep insight and practicality in saving sexless and struggling marriages. Athol's ability to divine the source of relationship difficulties and pose a practical solution is legendary.

Athol remained reluctant to advertise MMSL, yet word of mouth spread his expertise to the point where he was able to quit nursing and pursue MMSL full time in 2012. Always a theorist at heart, he spent a further year managing the MMSL forum of 1750 people and watching his advice play out in real time. The further insights gained resulted in *The Mindful Attraction Plan*, capping the cycle that MMSL started.

For Athol the publication of *The Mindful Attraction Plan comes* with a sense of peace after two decades of personal struggle for understanding. Ironically, Athol has come full circle and entered a de facto ministry of dispensing caring advice and true concern for others. He is a very bright, kind, honest, secular and spiritual man.

The Website

Find a Coach

The purpose of having a coach is finding someone who can mentor you through the process of acting on everything I've been talking about in this book.

A coach knows it's a process and meets you where you are.

A coach is a high-energy friend who helps lift you up.

A coach helps push you through your barriers to success.

A coach stops you from just talking about it and keeps you accountable to being active.

A coach helps you see the forest when you're lost in the trees.

A coach helps you connect to wisdom greater than yourself.

A coach gets you in the game with a better chance to win.

Visit www.mindfulattractionplan.com and we'll talk.

Athol's Other Books

The Married Man Sex Life Primer 2011 cherry picks the best ideas of books like "The Mystery Method", "No More Mr. Nice Guy", and the volatile online world of the Pickup Artist a.k.a. "Game" community and merges them with a solid grounding in evolutionary psychology, sociology, biology and behavior modification. The result is a strong, effective plan for men to create sexually exciting marriages for themselves and their wives.

How to Answer "Do These Pants Make My Ass Look Fat?" A collection of 101 brilliant and hilariously true short essays that everyone interested in love, sex and marriage needs to read. A fearless intellect coupled with a compassionate spirit, Athol ruthlessly tosses out the politically correct bath water but keeps the babies safe. At times controversial, at times wickedly funny, but always a powerful voice for love, marriage and hope.

The main blog is at www.marriedmansexlife.com

The MMSL forum is at http://marriedmansexlife.vanillaforums.com/

As an all-purpose warning, *The Mindful Attraction Plan* is Athol "writing as a gentleman". *Married Man Sex Life* material is Athol "writing as a street fighter". It's good writing, just a little rough and ready in places. It's certainly worth a read though.